D1217793

KINGDOM OF EARTH

(The Seven Descents of Myrtle)

By TENNESSEE WILLIAMS

PLAYS

Baby Doll (a screenplay)
Cat on a Hot Tin Roof
The Eccentricities of a Nightingale & Summer and Smoke
The Glass Menagerie
Kingdom of Earth (The Seven Descents of Myrtle)
The Milk Train Doesn't Stop Here Anymore
The Night of the Iguana
Orpheus Descending
Period of Adjustment
A Streetcar Named Desire
Suddenly Last Summer
Three Plays
The Rose Tattoo
Camino Real
Sweet Bird of Youth
27 Wagons Full of Cotton and Other Plays

POETRY

In the Winter of Cities

PROSE

Hard Candy and Other Stories
The Knightly Quest and Other Stories
One Arm and Other Stories
The Roman Spring of Mrs. Stone

KINGDOM OF EARTH

(The Seven Descents of Myrtle)

by TENNESSEE WILLIAMS

A NEW DIRECTIONS BOOK

Library of Congress Catalog Card Number: 68-28282

Manufactured in the United States of America.

New Directions Books are published for James Laughlin
by New Directions Publishing Corporation,
333 Sixth Avenue, New York 10014.

KINGDOM OF EARTH

(The Seven Descents of Myrtle)

Kingdom of Earth (The Seven Descents of Myrtle) was presented at the Ethel Barrymore Theatre in New York on March 27, 1968 by David Merrick. It was directed by José Quintero; the stage setting and lighting by Jo Mielziner; costumes by Jane Greenwood. The cast, in order of appearance, was as follows:

CHICKEN	HARRY GUARDINO
MYRTLE	ESTELLE PARSONS
LOT	BRIAN BEDFORD

SCENE ONE

At rise of the curtain, the stage set, uninhabited, has the mood of a blues song whose subject is loneliness. It is the back of a Mississippi Delta farmhouse, a story and a half high, its walls gray against a sky the same color. On either side of it stand growths of cane, half the height of the house, rattling in a moaning wind. Continually through these sounds is heard the low, insistent murmur of vast waters in flood or near it. This back wall of the house, except for a doorway, is represented by a scrim that will lift when the house is entered. Then the interior will be exposed: a kitchen to the right, a mysterious little "parlor" to the left, a narrow, dark hall between them: a flight of stairs to an upper hall and a low, slant-ceilinged bedroom to the left. The right side of the upper half-story is never used in the play and is always masked. It is a difficult set that requires the inventions of a very gifted designer. A few moments after the curtain rises, a car is heard approaching and stopping close by.

MAN'S VOICE: Hey, Chicken! Chicken!

[*There is a whine of wind. Then the one being called appears from offstage. He is a young man (30 or 35) in rubber hip boots covered with river slick. He seems a suitable antagonist to a flooding river.*]

WOMAN'S VOICE: We're clearin' out of our place.

CHICKEN: I see.

MAN'S VOICE: We're goin' up to Sunset. That's over the crest of the river.

CHICKEN: That's radio talk. I pay no attention to it.

WOMAN'S VOICE: Sorry we don't have room for you in our car.

CHICKEN: Never mind that. I wouldn't go if I had my own car to go in.

[*He is staring straight out as if the voices came from the back of the theatre. Dull lightning flickers about the gray place.*]

—So don't worry about it.

WOMAN'S VOICE [*turned openly malicious*]: I ain't worried about it, it's your worry, Chicken, but we got word that ole man Sikes might dynamite his south bank levee tonight to save his nawth bank levee, and if he does, this place of yours will be under at least ten foot of water, you know that.

CHICKEN [*raising his voice*]: I'd sooner be caught in my house by ten foot of water than caught in the mud on a road between here an' Sunset an' drown like kittens tied in a sack with rocks an' thrown in the river, cause anyhow in this house which is stood out five floods there's something I can climb onto, I can climb on the roof and set on the roof with the chickens till the water goes down. I done that before and can do it again, why, that's how I got my name Chicken, they named me Chicken because I set on the roof with the chickens one time this place was flooded.

WOMAN'S VOICE [*spitefully*]: A person could git awful hungry on a roof befo' the water wint down.

CHICKEN: Shit, if I got hungry I'd bite the haid off one of the other chickens and drink its blood.

MAN'S VOICE: I seen a man do that in a freak show once.

WOMAN'S VOICE: Chicken looks like he could do it, an' enjoy it. G'bye, Chicken. Daddy, le's go, we're cold.

[*Motor roars and splutters; the tires spin in the muck.*]

CHICKEN: Seems like you're stuck already. Sorry I don't have room fo' you in the house.

WOMAN'S VOICE: Sorry we don't have room fo' *you* in the car.

[*Tires catch*]

MAN'S VOICE: *Here we go!*

[*The sound of the car and bawling children fade out and we hear the muted warning of the river. The cane stalks make a sad rattling noise in the whining wind.* CHICKEN *enters kitchen and strikes a match; lights an oil lamp and warms his hands on its chimney as the glass gets hot. The flame makes grotesque shadows on his dark face. He is a strange-looking young man but also remarkably good-looking with his very light eyes, darker-than-olive skin, and the power and male grace of his body. After his hands are warmed up on the lamp chimney, he crosses with lamp to stove but on the way is distracted by a nude girl's body in a calendar picture, tacked directly over a disordered army cot pushed against kitchen wall. He turns the lamp up higher to see the picture more clearly, one hand at the same time falling involuntarily down his body. But he mutters sharply, "Nah!" and then goes on to the stove and cupboard. He starts preparing himself a pot of coffee, from time to time repeating the* WOMAN'S *mocking shout, "Sorry we don't have room for you in the car." After some moments he abruptly freezes, cocking his head like an animal at a warning sound. He listens for several beats before the audience can hear what he hears—the sound of an approaching motor. As the sound gets close to the house, he blows out the lamp and leans over it, as if glaring out a dim window in the open wall of the set. Then mutters sharply to himself—*]

CHICKEN: *Him!*

[*Motor stops nearby and a* WOMAN'S VOICE *is heard crying out something.* CHICKEN *grunts, astonished.*]

—Him and a *woman!*

[*He sets the lamp down quickly and runs to lock the door between the narrow, dark hall and the kitchen.* MYRTLE *and* LOT *appear downstage left, by the back door of the house. Neither is a person that could avoid curious attention.* MYRTLE *is a rather fleshy young woman, amiably loud-voiced. She is wearing a pink turtle-neck sweater and tight checkered slacks. Her blond-dyed hair is tied up in a wet silk scarf, magenta-colored. Her appearance suggests an imitation of a Hollywood glamor-girl which doesn't succeed as a good imitation.* LOT *comes on behind her, bearing two suitcases with great difficulty. He is a frail, delicately—you might say exotically—pretty youth of about twenty. He is ten years younger than* MYRTLE, *and his frailty makes him look even younger.* MYRTLE *dominates him in an amiable way.*]

MYRTLE: This here ain't the front door of the house.

LOT [*panting*]: No. Back.

MYRTLE: Well, then, you just march yourself around to the front door, then, cause I'm not about to enter my new home for th' first time by th' back door, No, Siree, I'm not!

[*Has already started around house, brushing through the canebrake.*]

I don't expect you to carry me over the threshold like you ought to but at least you don't have to take me in the back door.

[*Her complaint is affable, gay; she is enormously relieved that the dreadful journey is over safely.* MYRTLE *is a good-natured thing—almost ridiculously so. She has nothing else to meet the world with but good nature. . . . Her vigorous voice fades under the whine of wind.* LOT *draws a deep, difficult breath and attempts to follow her vigorous lead but can't make it: He staggers coughing against the rain-washed gray wall of the house, dropping his damp, cardboard suitcase.*

He leans panting against the wet frame wall as MYRTLE *calls to him from out front, above wind.*]

Hey, Lot, come awn!

[*Inside the dim kitchen, at a safe distance from the dusty windowpane in the imaginary fourth wall,* CHICKEN *is leaning stiffly over to look out and listen, like a crouched animal. He is muttering barely audibly to himself. After about ten beats,* MYRTLE *stops waiting out front and comes charging back around the side of the house, imitating the howl of the wind.*]

Woooo! Woooo! That wind is penetratin'! Sharp as a butcher's knife! What's holdin' you up back here?

LOT: No—breath—left . . .

[*She rushes up to him—an avalanche of motherly concern.*]

MYRTLE: Aw, baby, love!

LOT: Shouldn't have tried to carry—luggage . . .

[*He raises his pale, lost eyes to the fading-out sky above* MYRTLE's *look of concern.*]

MYRTLE: Well, I swan!

LOT [*breathlessly, with a touch of disdain*]: —What is swan, why swan?

MYRTLE: You'll have to ask my dead Granny, she always said "I swan."

LOT [*lowering his gaze to* MYRTLE]: To prove she wasn't a goose?

[*He bends, stiffly, to pick up a suitcase but* MYRTLE *snatches it from him.*]

MYRTLE: You come on and stop leaning against those cold, wet boards and let's get into our house!

[*She has the suitcase and is trying the back door, saying—*] This door is locked.

LOT: No. Just stuck, always sticks in wet weather.

[*She pulls, the door gives violently and she almost tumbles off the back steps. She recovers, laughing, and hauls the suitcase inside, heading straight up the dark, narrow hall.*]

LOT [*behind her*]: Where are you going?

MYRTLE: I'm goin' straight to the parlor. I want the parlor to be my first impression of my new home. Is this the door to the parlor?

LOT: Uh-huh.

MYRTLE: It's stuck, too. [*It gives before her weight.*] *There now!*

LOT: Go in.

MYRTLE: You go in and light the lights in that parlor so I can see it.

LOT [*pressing the switch*]: —The lights don't light.

MYRTLE: How come they don't light, baby?

LOT: Sometimes—[*He draws a deep breath.*] —when the river is flooding some places, the electric current that makes the lights light—[*He is talking to her as if she were mentally deficient. He draws another deep breath that wheezes in his throat.*] —is temporarily interrupted, Myrtle.

MYRTLE: How long is temporarily?

LOT: Oh, it comes back on when the— [*deep breath*] —water goes down. These drapes are velvet drapes—neglected lately.

[*He opens them as gently as if they had feeling. Fading gray light enters the parlor.*]

MYRTLE: —Well, this is an elegant parlor, an elegant little parlor.

LOT: My mother did all she could to give some quality to the place but my father— [*deep breath*] —was not just indifferent to the effort she made but opposed it. He was a man that liked to sit in a kitchen and wouldn't let Mother build a dining room onto the house. When he died, howling like a wild beast, Mother was free to transform this place or tear it down to the ground, but life was cruel to Mother. It gave her no time to carry out her plans.

MYRTLE: —She— ?

LOT: Outlived my father by shortly less than one year.

MYRTLE: —Sad . . .

LOT: —Yes. —Tragic.

MYRTLE: —Hmmm. A parlor with gold chairs is—like a dream!

LOT: The chandelier is crystal but the pendants are dusty, they've got to be all taken down, one by one, dipped in hot, soapy water. Then rinsed in a bowl of clear water, then dried off with soft tissue paper and hung back up.

[CHICKEN *grins savagely in the kitchen.*]

Mother and I used to do it, she never allowed the colored girl to touch a thing in this parlor or even come in it. Beautiful things can only be safely cared for by people that know and love them. The day before she died, do you know what she did?

[MYRTLE *shakes her head, staring curiously at her exotic young husband.*]

—She climbed a ladder in here and removed each crystal pendant from the little brass hook it hung on, passed it down to me, to be soaped and rinsed and dried, and then replaced on its little brass hook. "Son," she said to me, "help me down off this ladder, I don't know why I'm so tired."

MYRTLE: Baby, you got a mother complex, as they call it, and I'm gonna make you forget it. You hear me?

LOT: You've got a voice that no one in a room with you could help but hear when you speak.

MYRTLE: That's awright. When I speak I want to be heard. Now, baby, this mother complex, I'm gonna get that out of you, Lot, cause I'm not just your wife, I'm also your mother, and I'm not daid, I'm livin'. A-course I don't mean I'm gonna replace her in your heart, but—

[*She draws up one of the little gilded chairs close to the one on which he is seated.*]

LOT: Don't sit on mother's gold chairs. They break too easy.

MYRTLE: You are sittin' on one.

LOT: I'm lighter than you.

MYRTLE: Well! I stand corrected! —Mr. Skin and Bones! —Do I have to stay on my feet in this parlor or can I sit on the sofa?

LOT: Yes, sit on the sofa. [*Slight pause. His head droops forward and his violet-lidded eyes close.*] —The little animal has to make a home of its own. . . .

MYRTLE: I didn't catch that remark.

LOT: —What?

MYRTLE: You said something about an animal.

LOT: I'm too tired to know what I'm saying.

MYRTLE: Are you too tired to hear what *I'm* saying?

LOT: What are you saying?

MYRTLE: I'm saying that all my electric equipment is sitting out there under the leaky roof of your car.

LOT: —Oh. —Yes . . .

MYRTLE: Didn' you tell me you had niggers here working fo' you?

LOT: There's a house girl named Clara and her unmarried husband.

MYRTLE: How do you call this unmarried couple of niggers when you want something done?

LOT: You— [*deep breath*] —have to step outside and ring a bell for 'em.

MYRTLE: Where is this bell you ring for 'em?

LOT: The bell is— [*deep breath*] —in the kitchen.

MYRTLE: Well, kitchen here I come!

[*During the above,* CHICKEN *had opened the kitchen door to hear the talk in the parlor. Now he closes and locks the door silently.*]

The unmarried nigra couple're gonna step pretty lively fo' Mrs. Lot Ravenstock.

[*She charges to the kitchen door behind which* CHICKEN *is lurking.* LOT *sways and falls off the chair; staggers to the sofa.* MYRTLE *finds the door locked, rattles the knob and calls out—*]

Who is in there? Who is in this kitchen? —Somebody's in there!

[*She presses her ear to the door.* CHICKEN *breathes loudly as if he'd been fighting.* MYRTLE *rattles the knob again and a key falls to the floor inside the kitchen.* MYRTLE *is startled and subdued: she returns to the parlor as if a little frightened.*]

—If that's a dawg in there, why don't it bark?

LOT: —Dawg?

MYRTLE: That kitchen door was locked or it was stuck mighty tight. And I swear I heard something breathing right behind it, like a big dawg was in there. Then I rattled the knob and I heard a key fall to the floor. Will you wake up an' lissen t'what I tell you?

LOT [*hoarse whisper*]: I thought he was hiding in there.

MYRTLE: Who? What?

LOT: —Chicken. . . .

MYRTLE: Chicken? Hiding? A chicken, you say, is hiding in the kitchen? What are you tawkin about! —No chicken breathes that loud that I ever met!

LOT: Myrtle, when I say "Chicken" I don't mean the kind of chicken with feathers, I mean my half brother Chicken who runs this place for me.

MYRTLE: I'll be switched! This is a piece of news!

LOT: Keep your voice down, please. I got some things to tell you about the situation on this place.

MYRTLE: —Maybe you should've told me about it before?

LOT: Yes, maybe. But anyhow . . . now . . .

MYRTLE: You are making me nervous. You mean your brother is hiding in that kitchen while we are sitting in here half frozen?

LOT: Cain't you talk quiet?

MYRTLE: Not when I am upset. If he is in there, why don't you call him out?

LOT: He'll come out after while. The sight of a woman talking in this house must have give him a little something to think about in that kitchen, is what I figure.

MYRTLE: Well, all I can say is—"*Well!*"

LOT: —That's what I figure.

MYRTLE: And that's why you're shaking all over, not cause it's cold.

LOT: I'm shaking because I am cold with no fire anywhere in this house except in the kitchen. And it's locked up. With him in it.

MYRTLE: This makes about as much sense as a Chinese crossword puzzle to me, but maybe that long, wet ride has injured my brain. Can you explain to me why this half brother of yours would be hiding in the kitchen when we come home, pretending not to be here or— God knows what?!

LOT: Everything can't be explained to you all at once here, Myrtle. Will you try to remember something? Will you just try to get something in your haid?

MYRTLE: What?

LOT: This place is mine. You are my wife. You are now the lady of the house. Is that understood?

MYRTLE: Then why—?

LOT: Sh! Will you? Please? Keep your voice down to something under a shout?

MYRTLE: But—

LOT: Will you? Will you PLEASE?
[*Pause*]

MYRTLE: Awright. [*Sniffs*] Now I got the shivers, too. —If he's in the kitchen, why don't he come out?

LOT: Oh, he'll come out, after he's had three or four drinks in there to work up his nerve.

MYRTLE: You mean he's bashful?

LOT: He's strange by nature, and not accepted around here.

MYRTLE: I think we ought to go call him, it would be more natural to.

LOT: He won't come out till he's ready. Be patient. Do you like sherry wine?

MYRTLE: I don't think I ever had any.

LOT: Some of Miss Lottie's sherry's still left in this ole cut-glass decanter.

MYRTLE [*absently*]: Aw. Good. Good. . . .

LOT [*in his thin, breathless voice*]: This is Bohemian glass, these here wineglasses are.

MYRTLE: —What dya know. . . .

LOT: Ev'ry afternoon about this time, Miss Lottie would take a glass of this Spanish sherry with a raw egg in it to keep her strength up. It would always revive her, even when she was down to eighty-two pounds, her afternoon sherry and eggs, she called it her sherry flip, would pick her right up and she'd be bright an' lively.

MYRTLE: —Imagine me thinkin' that that was a dawg in there! Yeah, I thought that huffing I heard in there was a big old dawg in the kitchen, locked up in there. I didn't— Ha Ha!— suspect that it was— Ha Ha! —your—*brother*. . . .

[*He begins to cough: the cough shakes him like a dead leaf, and he leans panting against the wall staring at* MYRTLE *with pale, stricken eyes. She gathers him close in her arms*. . . .]

Why, baby! Precious love!— That's an *awful* cough! —I wonder if you could be comin' down with th' flu?

LOT: —Lissen! —He's movin' now!

[CHICKEN'*s frozen attitude by the door was released by the sound of* LOT'*s paroxysm of coughing: He crosses to a cupboard, takes out a jug and takes a long, long drink.*]

—A place with no woman sure does all go to pieces.

MYRTLE: Well, now they's a woman here.

LOT: That's right: we'll make some changes.

MYRTLE: You bet we will. And bright and early tomorrow, the first thing we do after breakfast, we'll, we'll, we'll! —We'll get out that ole stepladder and wash those whatcha-ma-call-ems and make them shine like the chandelier in Loew's State on Main Street in Memphis! And we will—oh, we'll do a whole lot of things as soon as this weather clears up. And soon it's going to be summer. You know that, Sugar? It's going to be summer real soon and—a small animal needs a place of its own.

LOT: Yeah, it'll be summer, the afternoons'll be long, the damp'll dry out of the walls and—

MYRTLE: I'M GONNA MAKE YOU REST! And build you up. You hear me? I'm gonna make you recover your lost strength, baby. —You and me are gonna have us a baby, and if it's a boy, we're going to call it Lot and if it's a girl we're gonna name her Lottie.

LOT [*his eyes falling shut*]: If beds could talk what stories they could tell. . . .

MYRTLE: Baby, last night don't count. You was too nervous. I'll tell you something I know that might surprise you. A man is twice as nervous as a woman and you are twice as nervous as a man.

LOT: Do you mean I'm not a man?

MYRTLE: I mean you're a man but superior to a man. [*Hugs him to her and sings—*]

"Cuddle up a little closer, baby mine.
Cuddle up and say you'll be my clinging vine!"

Mmmm, Sugar! Last night you touched the deepest chord in my nature which is the maternal chord in me. T'night I'm gonna cradle you in my arms, probably won't sleep, just watch you sleepin' an' hold you all night long, and it'll be better than sleep. Do you know, do you realize what a beautiful thing you are?

LOT: I realize that I resemble my mother.

MYRTLE: To me you resemble just *you.* The first, the most, the *only* refined man in my life. Skin, eyes, hair any girl would be jealous of. A mouth like a flower. Kiss me! [*He submits to a kiss.*] Mmmm. I could kiss you forever!

LOT: I wouldn't be able to breathe.

MYRTLE: You're refined and elegant as this parlor.

LOT: I want you to promise me something. If Chicken asks you, and when he gets drunk he will ask you—

MYRTLE: Chicken will ask me nothing that I won't answer in aces and spades.

LOT: There's something you mustn't answer if he asks you.

MYRTLE: What thing is that, baby?

LOT: If I'm a—

MYRTLE: If you're a what?

LOT: Strong lover. —Tell him I satisfy you.

MYRTLE: Oh, now, baby, there'd be no lie about that. Y'know, they's a lot more to this sex business than two people jumpin' up an' down on each other's eggs. You know that or you *ought* to.

LOT: I'm going to satisfy you when I get my strength back, and meanwhile—make out like I do. Completely. Already. I mean when talking to Chicken.

MYRTLE: Aw, Chicken again, a man that huffs like a dawg an' hides in the kitchen, do you think I'd talk about us to him, about our love with each other? All I want from that man is that he opens the kitchen door so I can go in there and grab hold of that bell and ring the clapper off it for that girl that works here, that Clara. I'll make her step, all right, and step quick, too. The first thing she's gotta do is haul in all that electric equipment settin' in the car, before it gits damp an' rusts on me.

LOT: Myrtle, I told you that when there's danger of flood, the colored help on a place cut out for high ground. —Till the danger's over.

MYRTLE: Then what're we doin' on low ground instid of high ground?

LOT: To protect our property from possible flood damage. This is your house, your home. Aren't you concerned with protecting it for us?

MYRTLE: My house, my home! I never known, I never even suspected, how much havin' property of my own could mean to me till all of a sudden I have some. House, home, land, a little dream of a parlor, elegant as you, refined as you are.

[*During this talk,* CHICKEN *has his ear pressed to the kitchen door, fiercely muttering phrases from the talk.*]

LOT: —Chicken calls me a sissy.

MYRTLE: Well, he better not call you no sissy when Myrtle's around. I'll fix his wagon up good, I mean I WILL!

LOT: SHH!—Myrtle, you've got an uncontrollable voice. He's listening to us.—You think you could handle Chicken?

MYRTLE: Want to make a bet on it? I've yet to meet the man that I couldn't handle.

LOT: You ain't met Chicken.

MYRTLE: I'm gonna meet him!—whin he comes outa that kitchen. . . .

LOT: He will, soon, now. It's gettin' dark outside and I heard him set the jug down on the kitchen table.

MYRTLE: Awright, I'm *ready* for him, anytime he comes out, I'm ready to meet him and one thing I want to git straight. Who's going to be running this place, me or this Chicken?

LOT: This place is mine. You're my wife.

MYRTLE: That's what I wanted to know. Then I'm in charge here.

LOT: You're taking the place of Miss Lottie. She ran the house and you'll run it.

MYRTLE: Good. Then that's understood.

LOT: It better be understood. Cause Chicken is not my brother, we're just half brothers and the place went to me. It's mine.

MYRTLE: Did you have diff'rent daddies?

LOT: No, we had diff'rent mothers. *Very* diff'rent mothers!

[CHICKEN *snorts like a wild horse*]

He's coming out now!

[CHICKEN *emerges slowly from the kitchen and starts up the dark, narrow hall.*]

MYRTLE: Yes. I hear him coming. Let's go meet him.

LOT: No. Wait here. Sit tight. And remember that you're the lady of the house.

[CHICKEN *pauses, listening in the dim hall.*]

MYRTLE: It don't seem natural to me.

[LOT *removes an ivory cigarette holder from a coat pocket, puts a cigarette in it and lights it. His hands are shaky.*]

[*nervously*] —A parlor with gold chairs is like a dream!

LOT: —A woman in the house is like a dream.

MYRTLE: —I must be hearing things.

LOT: What did you hear?

MYRTLE: I, I—thought I heard footsteps in the hall.

LOT: Human or animal footsteps?

[CHICKEN *opens the parlor door.*]

Aw. —Hello, Chicken. Don't come in the parlor till you take off those muddy boots.

[CHICKEN *disregards this instruction: enters the parlor.* MYRTLE *rises nervously but* LOT *remains seated, smiling icily through a cloud of cigarette smoke.*]

CHICKEN: They turn you loose from the hospital?

LOT: I wasn't locked in it. A hospital ain't a jail. I was dismissed.

CHICKEN: Couldn't do nothing more for you?

LOT: I was dismissed as cured.

CHICKEN: I see. And who is this woman?

LOT: You mean who is this lady. This lady is my wife. Myrtle, this is Chicken. Chicken, this is Myrtle.

CHICKEN: Why did you all come back here?

LOT: Wanted to is the reason.

CHICKEN: With this flood? In the county?

LOT: That's right. I wanted to see that my mother's things are taken out of the parlor before the downstairs is flooded.

CHICKEN: What good'll that do if the upstairs is flooded, too?

MYRTLE: Oh, my God, the flood won't go *that* high, will it?

CHICKEN: You don't know much about floods.

MYRTLE: All I know is I'm scared to death of deep water.

CHICKEN: Then how come you drove back here through that high water you must've hit south of Sunset?

MYRTLE: I begged Lot to turn back but he was bound an' determined to git us home, I couldn't stop him, he was determined to make it.

CHICKEN: Wanta know something? This time tomorrow, both floors of this house will be full of floodwater.

[MYRTLE *draws a long, noisy breath of dismay and terror.*]

The river gauge is thirty-two foot of water at Friar's Point and the crest is still above Memphis. And I just got word from those sons of bitches, Potters, that ole man Sikes is about to blow up the south end of his levee to save the rest of it, he's planning to dynamite it tonight and you—come home just in time for it.

MYRTLE: Lot, baby, I think we ought to turn right around and drive back.

LOT: No. We're home. We're not gonna leave here. Chicken's just tryin' to scare us. Why don't you leave, Chicken, if you're scared of the flood?

CHICKEN: I ain't about to leave here. You know we got this agreement. Have you forgotten about the agreement we signed between us?

LOT: That was before I got married. Now I am.

CHICKEN [*to* MYRTLE]: Are you his nurse?

MYRTLE: Why, no, I'm Mrs. Lot Ravenstock and have been Mrs. Lot Ravenstock since yesterday mawnin.

CHICKEN: I know of invalid men to marry their nurses, or anyhow live with 'em like they was married.

MYRTLE: We're married, and I wasn't a nurse. Y'know, I don't think I ever seen so little resemblance between two brothers.

CHICKEN: We're half brothers.

LOT: Chicken's much darker complected. Don't you notice?

MYRTLE: There's so little light in the room.

CHICKEN: I work out in the fields and Lot just lays in bed.

LOT:—I'd like some hot coffee, now.

CHICKEN: Coffee's in the kitchen. [*He returns to the kitchen.*]

MYRTLE: Git up, Lot. Come along.

LOT [*remaining on sofa*]: How does he impress you?

MYRTLE: I wouldn't call that man a pleasant surprise, and I don't understand why you never mentioned him to me so I'd be a little prepared, but—

LOT: Don't let him scare you.

MYRTLE: I'm not scared of that man, or any man livin'! No, sir!

CHICKEN [*at kitchen door*]: Decided y'don't want coffee?

MYRTLE: Be right there.

LOT [*staggering up from the sofa*]: If he sees he can bluff an' bully you, that's what he'll do, so remember—we're two against one in this house and the house is ours.

[*They go hand in hand to the kitchen.* CHICKEN *sets tin cups on the table.*]

—Myrtle an' I'll have our coffee in china cups.

CHICKEN: The china cups all broke.

LOT: You broke Mother's china cups?

MYRTLE: Lot, baby, china breaks, nobody breaks it on purpose unless there's a fight. This is—I like our kitchen. All but that nakid girl's pitcher on the wall there. I could do without that.

CHICKEN: Jealous of her?

MYRTLE: I think it's pitiful of a strong, grown man like you to pleasure yourself like a kid with that kind of pitcher. I don't have to ask if you're a bachelor now.

CHICKEN: Lot an' me are bachelors, both of us.

MYRTLE: You're a bachelor but my baby ain't.

CHICKEN: Your baby's more of a bachelor than me.

MYRTLE: I'm here to prove he ain't.

CHICKEN: Hmm. I didn't catch your name.

MYRTLE: My maiden name was Myrtle Kane, but now it's legally changed to Mrs. Lot Ravenstock.

CHICKEN: How long've you been Lot's nurse?

MYRTLE: I am nobody's nurse. To repeat that statement.

LOT: We've been married two days, almost.

MYRTLE: My girl-friend, Georgia, said I was robbin' the cradle, you know, cradle snatchin'.

[*No response to her laugh.*]

And I had always boasted that I was too practical-minded for love at first sight but practicality flew out the window whin this boy come in. —I want you to know it turned my bones to water!

LOT: Chicken, we'll have some coffee.

CHICKEN: Pour some out of the coffeepot on the stove.

[*He stares steadily at* MYRTLE.]

So you're in the—nursin' profession?

LOT: Myrtle was in show business.

MYRTLE: Why do you keep askin' if I'm a nurse? Oh, I once did a little of what they call practical nursing, took care of a feeble person till he died on me, out of kindness—sympathy. . . .

[*She is pouring coffee into three tin cups.*]

Is everyone's name in the pot? The coffee's still hot.

CHICKEN: Yeah. Show business, huh?

MYRTLE: I've hed all kinds of employment in my life. Respectable employment.

[*She laughs genially and gives* CHICKEN *a playful little slap on the shoulder.*]

Oh, in my life I've taken the sweets with the sours, and it's been smooth as silk in my experience and other times rough as a cob. Yais, I've known both in my time. However, I've kept my haid above water, that I can say for myself, and I've rowed my own boat, too. Never had to depend on another soul. No, sir. I've pulled my own weight in this world. Here is my right hand to God, if you don't believe me, and nothing, nobody, never has made me bitter. No sir! What all have I done? I'll tell you all that I've done in my life, and that's a-plenty, yes, siree, a-plenty.

LOT: Myrtle?

MYRTLE: Huh? What, baby?

LOT: I think it's time to bring in that carload of electric equipment.

MYRTLE: Your brother 'n' me'll do that, don't worry about it. Your brother wants to know what all I've done in my life, and I'm gonna tell him. You might find it int'restin', too.

LOT: Yes, I might, if I hadn't already heard it.

[*He sinks into a chair and his eyes fall shut. His eyelids are violet. He sways a little as if he might fall from the chair.*]

MYRTLE: I'll just hit the high spots, baby. Whin I was fifteen I worked as operator of a Photo-matic machine on the beach at Galveston, Texas. I been—you won't believe this but it's true as I'm standin' here before you!—I been the headless woman in a carnival show. All a fake, done with mirrors! Sat in a chair and pretended to have no haid, it was done with mirrors! But completely convincin'!

LOT: Myrtle, skip to show business.

MYRTLE: Baby, that was show business, my first experience in it and it's where my heart still belongs.

CHICKEN: —What is she talkin' about?

LOT [*as if asleep*]: Myrtle was in show business.

CHICKEN: Hunh?

LOT: [*rousing a bit*]: Show him that picture of "The Four Hot Shots from Mobile."

MYRTLE: Oh, that ole snap, that ole publicity still, I wonder if I still got it.

LOT: You showed it to me a minute after we met.

MYRTLE: I'll see if I still got it on me.

LOT: You put it back in your handbag.

MYRTLE: Pandora's box!

CHICKEN: Whose box?

MYRTLE [*a bit nervously*]: Cups refilled with coffee. Now let me lead a parade back into that elegant little parlor and I'll show you and tell you about the Four Hot Shots from Mobile. Come along, follow me, boys. . . .

[*She has put the tin cups of coffee on a plate: marches into the parlor and sets the plate down on a table before the couch.* LOT *and* CHICKEN *are still in the kitchen.*]

CHICKEN: Only a lunatic would marry you and you sure have found the right party.

LOT: Is the black bird of jealousy eating at your heart, Chicken?

MYRTLE: Boys, I've found the pitcher of the Four Hot Shots from Mobile and I'm waiting to show it to you.

CHICKEN: She wants you to get up out of the chair and go in Miss Lottie's parlor if you can.

LOT: Sure I can. Without trouble.

[*He gets up and falls to his knees.* CHICKEN *laughs and sets him on his feet.*]

CHICKEN: Able to walk or do you have to be carried?

LOT: The long trip made my dizzy.

MYRTLE: *Boys!*

CHICKEN: I bet there's a buzzard circlin' over the house, since you got here.

[*He turns away from* LOT *and goes to the parlor.* LOT *leans on the kitchen table a moment. Then gathers a bit of strength and follows into the parlor.* MYRTLE *has had no trouble at all in finding the "publicity still." She gazes at the photograph with a beguilement that it has never failed to give her.* CHICKEN *enters the parlor. She turns to him with a warm smile, extending the photo to him.* CHICKEN *takes it from her and regards it with considerable interest. Consciously or not, he drops one of his large, dusky hands over his crotch, which is emphasized, pushed out, by his hip boots.*]

MYRTLE: Well, there you are, here we are!

[LOT *sits carefully down on one of the "little gold chairs."*]

Here we are outside the Dew Drop Inn—in the live town of Tallahassee, F-L-A! It's in color, you see.

CHICKEN: Yes, I can see color. Where's these hot shots now, gone back to Mobile?

MYRTLE: —You ast me a sad question, where's them girls. You know somethin'? [*She is sincerely distressed.*]

CHICKEN: I know lots of things but I won't know *that* till you tell me.

MYRTLE: [*blows her nose and dabs at her eyes*]: From right to left. This tall redhead they called The Statuesque Beauty. [CHICKEN *grunts—but with interest.*] —her mutilated corpse was found under a trestle three years ago this Spring. [CHICKEN *grunts again.*] Don't that break your heart?

CHICKEN: No.

MYRTLE: Some one, some pervert I reckon, had cut her up with a knife, writ up in all the papers, you must've heard about it. I'm telling you it just about broke my heart, she was full of vim, vigor and vitality. And *fun?* The Statuesque Beauty was a continual circus.

CHICKEN: Unh. Circus quit now.

MYRTLE: This one next to her, sweet thing, still in her teens, billed as The Gulf Coast Blaze—a victim of a illegal operation.

CHICKEN: Daid?

MYRTLE [*blowing her nose again*]: Not livin', brother, bless her old sweet soul. And this one next to her, billed as The Texas Explosion, somehow I feel that her end was saddest of all. Devoured a full bottle of sleeping pills one night in a Wichita, Kansas hotel.

CHICKEN: Suicide, huh?

MYRTLE: Well, brother, you don't devour a full bottle of sleeping pills with much expectation of getting up early to-morrow. Oh, and this one, my God, The Midnight Stawm!— She wint on drugs. Y'see, all of us four girls lived in the same little frame house t' share expenses, y'know, and, well, one night I happened to be passin' down th' hall outside the bedroom of The Midnight Stawm. I smelt a strong smell of incense. I knocked at The Midnight Stawm's door and this strange voice called out "Who's there?" "Me, Myrtle." "Aw, you, come in." So in I wint, and she was sittin' there smokin' this thin cigarette with incense burnin' beside her. "What're you smokin'? "I'm smokin' grass," she answered, "have a stick with me, Myrtle." But instink tole me not to.

LOT: I'm tired, let's go up now.

MYRTLE [*hugging him to her*]: Rest on Myrtle, baby, and lemme finish the story. At that time, in Mobile, I was totally ignorant thin of things like that, but I had a suspicion that something had gone wrong with The Midnight Stawm.

CHICKEN: Aw?

MYRTLE: She'd took the first step to what she finally come to. So we other girls an' me, we talked it over and regretfully hed to ask The Midnight Stawm to give up her room there with us. Painful, very. But we didn't want the house raided. We were clean-livin' girls, as you'd hope to find in show business. —Here is me, The Petite Personality Kid that had all the luck in that outfit, and even her luck come mighty close to petering out once or twice, but character saved me.

CHICKEN: You are The Petite Personality Kid?

MYRTLE: That's how they billed me, brother.

CHICKEN: Built you?

MYRTLE: No, no, billed, not built. It's a term in show business meaning the name by which you're introduced to the public.

CHICKEN: You been introduced to the public?

MYRTLE: Yes, many times, many places. [*Returns snapshot to patent-leather purse.*]

CHICKEN:—How did the public like it? [*He gives her a slow, wolfish grin, his eyes appraising her body.*] —Did they yell "take it off" or did they yell "keep it on?"

[MYRTLE *laughs heartily but with a note of uncertainty.*]

LOT: Myrtle has a personality that the public responds to.

CHICKEN: Aw?

LOT: She received an ovation on TV. I saw it, I heard it. I was there to audition as—[*draws a long, painful breath*] —MC for a— "Tonight in Memphis" show. . . .

CHICKEN: Did the public respond to you, too?

LOT: —I —was —interviewed, and—
[*He shrugs slightly and puts a cigarette in an ivory holder.*]

CHICKEN: After this interview, you thought you'd do better back here? With a stripper to nurse you?

MYRTLE: Now, I don't like that, that's a little uncalled for!

CHICKEN: Did I say something wrong?

LOT: You said something wrong and offensive.

MYRTLE: It's my personality that I sell to the public—mainly.

CHICKEN: Yes, I bet. You kick with the right leg, you kick with the left leg, and between your legs you make your living?

MYRTLE: —Some remarks I deliberately don't hear!

LOT: Chicken, now that I'm home, in *my* home, on *my* land, with *my* wife, filthy talk has got to stop around here, I don't care if it means us getting along without you.

CHICKEN: Aw, you want me to go, now.

MYRTLE: Lot baby didn't mean that!

CHICKEN: What did "Lot baby" mean?

MYRTLE: All he means was we're sittin' here in this elegant little parlor under a crystal glass chandelier and Lot feels and I feel, too, that we should all talk and act like gentlemen an' — ladies!

LOT: I want to go up to bed, while I still have strength to.

CHICKEN: Your nurse'll carry you up.

MYRTLE: Lot, show your brother we're married, let him see the license.

[*Lot produces a paper.*]

CHICKEN: Shit, you can buy those things for two bits in a novelty store to show in a motel where you brought a woman to lay.

MYRTLE: This marriage license is genuine and if you doubt my word for it, call up the TV station in Memphis where we were married.

LOT: Myrtle and I were married on television yesterday morning.

CHICKEN: That statement makes no more sense than if you told me you licked TB and've got the strength of a mule team.

MYRTLE: Want to hear the whole story?

CHICKEN: I like to hear a good joke.

MYRTLE: Brother, this is no joke!

LOT: Let me lie down on this sofa.

MYRTLE: Lie down, baby, and rest your head in my lap while I tell your brother what happened to me in Memphis two days ago.

[LOT *reclines on the sofa with his head in* MYRTLE*'s lap. As she tells her story, she strokes his forehead and hair.*]

To start at the beginning, my luck had run out, you know luck does that sometimes, it peters out on you no matter how hard you try and decent and clean you live and close you are to your Saviour. Trials come in a lifetime and you got to face and accept them till the wheel of fortune turns again your way.

CHICKEN: Make this story short.

MYRTLE: Awright, day before yestiddy I happened to be on the street in Memphis for no particular reason and I seen this long line of people, all wimmen, and I said to myself these people are waiting for something, and if that many people are standing in line for something, it must be good.

CHICKEN: Uh-huh. Get on with the story.

MYRTLE: Well, I fell in the line-up with these other ladies and suddenly, all at once, this little Jewish type man come bolting out and hollered, "Ladies, the studio's full, no more admissions today." Everybody went "Awwwww," disappointed, but I said, "Mister, I don't know what this is but I want in on this thing, I been standing here two hours and I want in on this thing, whatever it is!" —I had him by the arm. He give me a funny look, he must've seen something in me, and he said, "Girlie, you just watch where I go and follow me fast as you can without attracting attention." He sort of whispered this to me out of the side of his mouth. So I stepped out of the line. I seen him bustling into a little alleyway back of the TV studio. I followed him around there and in a fire-escape door, and you know where I found myself? On a TV stage! And there I was, right there, right smack in the middle of a TV show, and this nice little plump little man, he had me by the elbow with such a tight grip I don't think a greased alligator could of got loose, and the first I known, d'ya know what I was doin'?

CHICKEN: Hustlin' a fast buck or two?

MYRTLE: I was standin' in front of a mike with cameras and lights on me, telling my story, broadcasting my woes to the world. I started to cry and everyone started to laugh, the studio rocked with 'em laughing. Why, when I was in show business as The Personality Kid, if I'd ever rocked a club like I rocked that TV public, I would, I bet you, hed hed my name in white lights on Broadway, that's the truth, I would of!

CHICKEN: Come to the point of the story if there is one.

MYRTLE: I sobbed and cried and it made me mad that they laughed. Y'know how mad it makes you to pour your heart out at someone an' have him mock you? Well, then I cut loose, I let 'em have it, I hollered out "What's so funny?" And then this little man that had ushered me in the back way, he whispered something to the MC of the show, and to my shock and astonishment a moment later I was led up to and set down on a golden throne and a big gold jewelled crown was set on my haid and the MC shouted to the audience, all applauding, "Hail to the Queen! All hail!" [*She makes a grand gesture.*] "All hail to thee, Queen of the Day!

LOT: Myrtle, condense the story.

MYRTLE [*oblivious to his suggestion*]: WELL! —I'm telling you, brother, I could have dropped through that stage floor to the boiler-room in the basement, whin I realized, that accidentally, just out of the blue, that I hed been chosen, selected as queen for nothing more or less than pouring out my heart to a room full of strangers.

LOT: I was there in that room.

MYRTLE: Yais, that's right, my blessed baby was there. Now then. I was given two choices, to be the "Hollywood-Queen-for-a-Day" or the "Take-Life-Easy Queen."

CHICKEN: This is a bitch of a story.

MYRTLE: Yais, ain't it! Now the "Hollywood-Queen-for-a-Day" is sent to Hollywood, first class on a plane, provided with a sport ensemble for daytime and a formal for night and has her hair styled by the hair stylist for the stars, and she spends eight hours hobnobbing with screen celebrities in famous places. On the other hand, the "Take-Life-Easy Queen" gets a small fortune in electric household equipment. Well, like ev'ry girl in show business, and many out of it, too, Hollywood was my dream, but—

LOT: Tell him why you switched and how we got married on a national hook-up.

MYRTLE: That's what I'm working up to.

CHICKEN: You're working up to it slowly.

MYRTLE: Give me patience, you want to know how this happened!

CHICKEN: Not if it takes till midnight.

MYRTLE: I'm leading up to the climax which is the climax of my life. I hed naturally chosen to be the Hollywood-Queen-for-a-Day and the ceremony was just about finished when somebody touches my arm. I turn around, still in my robe and crown, and there was my precious baby, completely unknown to me then. Gold-haired, soft-voiced, appealing. It was love-at-first-sight, immediate as a surprise, bang, right between my eyes. "Can I have your autograph, please?" is what he said to me. In that instant the love bug hit me, cupid's arrow shot a bull's eye in my heart. We made a date. On this date he said the love bug had bit him too, love-at-first-sight for us both. I phoned the TV studio and told 'em what had happened and I was going to git married and for that reason could I switch to being the Take-It-Easy-Life-Queen with all that electric equipment to start out with. There was no objection but there was a suggestion. "How would you and your husband-to-be like to be married on TV? In a lace bride's gown with a bouquet of lillies?"

LOT: That's the story. Yesterday we were married on TV.

CHICKEN: You acted out a make-believe marriage to fool the public, huh?

MYRTLE: If it wasn't a genuine marriage it sure fooled us.

LOT: It was a genuine marriage performed by a famous revivalist preacher.

MYRTLE: No more disagreeable talk. Back to the kitchen fo' the bell!

[*She rushes back to the kitchen and snatches up a cowbell on the table. Returns to parlor with it.*]

Is this the bell you ring fo' th' unmarried colored couple?

[CHICKEN *turns to give her a slow, blank look.*]

I am goin' out an' ring this bell and they are gonna bring in my 'lectric equipment before it rusts on me. I got a, I got a— 'lectric washer, two of 'em, one fo' clo'se and one for dishes,

I got a, I got a—'lectric home permanent set, 'lectric heater an' blanket an' a table model radio-TV set, so many 'lectric appliances we hardly had room enough for 'em in the car. You'll see whin that unmarried couple hauls them in here t' be dried off, an' connected.

CHICKEN: Yeah, I'll see. Go out an' ring the bell. Ring it loud and long, they don't hear good from a distance.

[MYRTLE *goes out on the back steps and rings the bell while* CHICKEN *and* LOT *stare silently at each other. She rings the bell loud and long but the only response is moaning wind and a dull flicker of lightning.*]

LOT [*finally speaking*]: Well, I guess I surprised you.

CHICKEN: You got a bigger surprise comin' to you.

LOT: What do you mean by that?

CHICKEN: If I said what I mean by it, it wouldn't be as big a surprise to you, would it?

[MYRTLE *returns.*]

MYRTLE: I rang an' rang an' got no answer out there.

CHICKEN: Don't let that bother you much. I don't think you all could git it on the roof whin the floodwater fills the house.

LOT: Stop talking about a flood to scare my wife.

MYRTLE: I don't and I can't believe a man would stay in this house if he really thought it was going to be flooded, so I'm not a-tall scared. Now who's going to help me bring in my prizes in the car?

CHICKEN: Your TV husband will do that.

LOT: Chicken will bring it in.

CHICKEN: Oh, no, Chicken won't.

MYRTLE: Thank you both very kindly. I'll bring in what I can carry without your help.

[*She goes out and off.*]

LOT: Help her with it. If you still work on the place.

CHICKEN: I will like shit.

LOT: Let's make an effort to forget what's past and work out a— decent— future.

CHICKEN: There's no future for you. I talked to your doctor before I made out that paper. You remember that agreement between us, witnessed, signed, notarized, giving the place to me when you take the one-way trip to the kingdom of heaven? I never have that paper out of my wallet in here. [*He taps the pocket of his leather jacket.*] —I was curious to know how long I might have to wait. I got your Memphis doctor on the phone to ask about the condition of your lungs. One's gone, he told me, and the other one's going. Limit: six months. Now passed.

[MYRTLE *rushes back into the house with a load of portable electric equipment.*]

MYRTLE: I carried in what I can carry and will get some help to bring the heavy stuff in.

[*She enters the parlor: the men ignore her. She sets the electric stuff down, as if she'd forgotten it, observing the tension between the two men. Sad, dull lightning quivers about the house.*]

CHICKEN: Didn't you tell this woman how you bleed?

MYRTLE: Bleed, Lot, baby? Bleed?

CHICKEN: Yeah, Lot baby bleeds. He bleeds like a chicken with its head chopped off. I'm Chicken, he's headless Chicken. Yes, he bleeds, he bleeds. But no, he don't have TB: He just makes a blood donation to Red Cross, only Red Cross is not quick enough to catch it in a—bucket. . . .

[LOT *suddenly springs forward, striking fiercely at* CHICKEN. CHICKEN *pushes him almost gently to the floor.* LOT *crawls groaning to his feet and staggers into hall and starts to drag himself up the steep, dark, narrow steps.*]

MYRTLE: I don't understand! What is it?

CHICKEN [*mimicking her*]: "I don't understand! What is it?"

MYRTLE [*backing up steps*]: You scare me!

CHICKEN: "You scare me!"

MYRTLE [*running up a few more steps*]: I'm going up with Lot!

CHICKEN: "I'm going up with Lot!"

[*She draws a gasping breath and scrambles up the narrow steps to the bedroom door that* LOT *has entered.* MYRTLE *comes up behind him and clings to his arm.*]

MYRTLE: I never been so terrified in my life!

LOT [*sadly, reflectively, his eyes searching the dim sky*]: Chicken says my doctor said—I'm dying!

MYRTLE: He mocked everything I said, he just stood there and mocked everything I said!

LOT: Can you imagine that? I'm going to die!

MYRTLE: Oh, let's go back, let's drive right back to Memphis!

LOT: —We can't, Myrtle.

MYRTLE: Why can't we? Why can't we drive back?

LOT: I'm going to die, that's why. . . .

[*He glances at her with a soft, surprised, rueful laugh. The scene dims out.*]

INTERMISSION.

SCENE TWO

The upstairs bedroom is lighted by an oil lamp. Late dusk surrounds the house, the "apple green dusk" of an evening clearing after rain which has just stopped. Water is heard running busily along tin gutters, down a spout and into a big mossy barrel beside the back door. Bullfrogs and possibly some crickets are making their forlorn and desultory comments, desultory as the forlorn talk in the bedroom where MYRTLE *is washing out some things at the rose-bud-printed washbowl and where* LOT *is in a rocker facing the audience at an angle; the chair is one of those wicker rockers that they have, or used to have, on verandahs of old-fashioned summer hôtels in the South. And* LOT*'s fair head, delicately pretty as a girl's, leans against a souvenir pillow from Biloxi. The pillow is made of green satin, the same as the counterpane on the brass bed. The aura of its former feminine occupant,* LOT*'s mother, still persists in this bedroom: a lady who liked violets and lace and mother-of-pearl and decorative fringes on things. . . .* LOT *is smoking with his long ivory holder;* MYRTLE *is wringing out some nylons as the curtain rises. She glances, from time to time, at her bridegroom as an uneasy scientist might glance at a test tube whose contents had turned an unexpected color. . . . All during this scene between* LOT *and* MYRTLE, CHICKEN *is seen in the very dim-lit kitchen, carving something into the kitchen table with a switch-blade knife—on his face a wolfish grin.*

MYRTLE: I wish I knew what was going on back of that long ivory cigarette holder and that Mona Lisa smile.

LOT: I got them both from my mother.

MYRTLE: Yes, well, regardless of where you got 'em, they baffle me. We been up here about two hours, I reckon, and all you've said to me is, "I'm dyin', Myrtle." When a couple has been married for twenty or thirty years it's natural for them to fall into long-drawn silences between them because they've talked themselves out, but you and me have been married for less than two days.

LOT: Why didn't you say something to me? I would've answered.

MYRTLE: Thanks. That's a comforting piece of news. —I didn't speak till you lit a cigarette because I thought you'd fallen asleep in that rocker.

LOT: No. I was sitting here thinking.

MYRTLE: I was standin' here thinkin', too, while I washed my nylons and undies.

LOT: Tell me your thoughts, Myrtle.

MYRTLE: I'll tell you one of 'em. Do you think you played fair and square with me when you brought me down here without a word of warning about that man, that animal, down there?

LOT: I thought it was better not to mention Chicken.

MYRTLE: Better for who? For you!

LOT: Yes, for me. You might not've come down here and I couldn't come down here alone.

MYRTLE: Selfishness in your nature isn't a thing to brag of.

LOT: No. I wasn't bragging.

MYRTLE: Every car, truck, wagon, crowds of people on foot headed the opposite way, and you wouldn't turn back! Can you give me a reasonable reason for that?

LOT: —I guess—

MYRTLE: What do you guess?

LOT: I guess I thought in my heart what Chicken told me and wanted to die in this bedroom where I was born. Yes, selfish as hell, but when people are desperate, Myrtle, they only think of themselves.

MYRTLE: Some people. Not all.

LOT: Some people—including me. —Don't hate me for it.

MYRTLE: Whin I love I don't hate.

LOT: You don't have a complex nature. —What time is it, Myrtle?

MYRTLE: My watch don't run. I just wear it now as a bracelet.

LOT: You wound it too tight and broke the springs?

MYRTLE: No, no, baby. Last Fourth of July I wint to a Shriners' picnic on a lake and a couple of drunk Shriners thought it was very funny to throw me in a lake with my watch on, so the works rusted.

LOT: What you should've done to prevent the works from rusting was to take it directly to a jewellers' shop and have the works removed and soaked in oil over-night.

MYRTLE [*sadly*]: I should of done many things in my life which I neglected t'do, and not soaking my watch in oil is not the most important I can think of.

LOT: You mean what you regret most is getting married to a —a impotent one-lung sissy who's got one foot in the grave and's about to step in with the other.

MYRTLE: You're putting words in my mouth that I wouldn't speak to anybody I love!

[*She has removed her slacks and is getting into a sheer blouse sprinkled with tiny brilliants and a velveteen skirt.*]

LOT: What're you dressing up for?

MYRTLE: I never keep on slacks after six p.m.

LOT: That outfit you're getting into looks like a costume.

MYRTLE: Baby, all of my dresses are made over from costumes.

LOT [*slowly with little pauses for breath*]: This particular one wasn't made over enough to prevent it from still looking like a costume.

MYRTLE: That could be so or not so, but I think it's a sweet little outfit.

LOT: One girl's opinion.

MYRTLE: Yais, an' trusted by her—with your permission.

LOT: I'm not in a position to give or not give permission.

MYRTLE: Lot? Baby? When people are under the weather, it often has the effeck of makin' 'em too critical or sarcastic.

LOT: My mother subscribed to *Vogue* and we both read it. I know the secret of dressing well is to dress in a way that's appropriate to the occasion.

MYRTLE: What occasion is this? Can you tell me?

LOT: It could be the end of the world, but even then—that almost ankle-length imitation velvet skirt might not be appropriate to it.

MYRTLE: This ain't the end of the world, God help me, Jesus, and this skirt is washable velvet.

LOT: There is no such thing as real velvet that's washable, Myrtle.

MYRTLE: Well, I swan, you talk like a dressmaker, Baby.

LOT: My mother, Miss Lottie, had a sense of style that a Paris designer might envy.

MYRTLE: If you talk about her much more, you'll turn me aginst her, Lot.

LOT: —That wouldn't matter. She doesn't exist any more. . . .

MYRTLE: All this style thet she hed, wasn't it wasted down here?

LOT: No, strangely no. In spite of my father who had the taste of a hawg, who ate with his hands and wiped them on his trousers, my mother, Miss Lottie, was socially accepted by sev'ral families with standing in Two River County.

MYRTLE: With so much style, accepted instid of refused, why did she marry this hawg?

LOT: That's a question I can no more answer than if you asked me why God made little green apples.

MYRTLE [*opening closet door in the back wall of the bedroom*]: I see, UH-HUH, well, tomorrow, baby, you or me or both of us is gonna clear your mother's clothes outa this closet so I don't have to live out of a suitcase.

LOT: —I'm sorry, but tomorrow—

[*He doesn't complete the sentence.* MYRTLE*'s attention is diverted by the loud sound of* CHICKEN *pushing his chair back from the kitchen table. He gets up and starts chopping potatoes into a hot skillet, dousing them with grease out of a can on the stove, and tossing into the skillet some strips of bacon. During the bedroom dialogue, he will pick out the fried bacon and eat it, all of it, and wipe his fingers on the seat of his pants.* LOT *coughs, rackingly.* MYRTLE *feels his forehead.*]

MYRTLE: That's a mean cough you got there, and I don't need a thermometer to tell me you're runnin' a fever, Baby. Yes, Sir, burnin' up with it!

LOT [*gasping*]: Fever is—the body's protection—reaction—to the enemy in it—any kind of—infection. . . .

MYRTLE: Sometimes you talk over my head. —I love you, precious baby, I love you and I'm here to protect and care for you, always! [*She presses her head to his.*]

LOT: Love me but don't smother me with it, Myrtle.

MYRTLE: —What a mean thing to say!

LOT: I didn't mean it that way. I meant I have trouble breathing and when you crouch over me like that, it makes it harder for me to draw my breath, that's all.

[*He puts another cigarette in the ivory holder. She snatches the holder away from him.*]

—Give that holder back to me!

MYRTLE: The last thing you need is to smoke!

LOT: It makes no difference now!

MYRTLE: It does to me!

LOT: If you don't return my holder, I'll smoke without it and nobody's going to stop me—at the end of the world. . . .

MYRTLE: Here! Take it back and drive a nail in your coffin but don't talk to me about the end of the world, I haven't come to it yet and don't intend to!

LOT: Thank you, Myrtle.

MYRTLE: Never talk that way to your wife that loves you, my precious blond-headed baby.

LOT: —I'm no more blond than you are.—My hair is bleached.

MYRTLE [*shocked*]: Did you say your hair is—bleached?

LOT: As bleached as yours. But I do a better job on my hair than you do on yours because my mother taught me. Ev'ry morning of the world, and if I'm alive tomorrow I'll do it again, I get up, brush my teeth and obey the calls of nature, and the next thing I do, in the hospital or out, is put a wad of cotton on the tip of an orange stick and dip it into a bottle and rub the roots of my hair so it never shows dark, and I don't use peroxide, I use a special formula which my mother invented and passed on to me. She said with blue eyes and fair skin, I'd look best as a blond, the same as she did. . . .

MYRTLE [*aghast*]: Well, I'll be switched. . . .

LOT: Now you're disillusioned with your young husband?

MYRTLE: —I thought at least I had married a natural blond.

LOT: Don't let it throw you and don't imagine you have married a fairy.

MYRTLE: Such an idea would never— [*leaves the statement in air*]

LOT: You've married someone to whom no kind of sex relation was ever as important as fighting sickness and trying with his mother to make, to create, a little elegance in a corner of the earth we lived in that wasn't favorable to it.

MYRTLE: —I—

LOT: —You what?

MYRTLE: —Understand. And I'm going to devote myself to you like a religion, mystery as you are, back of that ivory holder and Mona Lisa smile.

[*Pause.* CHICKEN *turns up the lamp in the kitchen and blows on the inscription he has carved into the kitchen table, grins at it. Then carries the lamp to the back wall of the kitchen and peers at the photo-in-color of a nude girl, tacked to the wall. —After a moment, he crosses into the hall and calls out—*]

CHICKEN: Hey, up there, Myrtle, Mrs. Lot Ravenstock. Ain't you all getting hungry for something besides each other?

MYRTLE: Should I answer that man?

LOT: Answer him if you're hungry.

MYRTLE [*calling down from the upper hall*]: Lot needs feeding and I could eat something, too.

CHICKEN: Come on down, then.

MYRTLE: All right, thank you, I will.

CHICKEN [*lowering his voice*]: Come down in a show costume and put on a show.

[MYRTLE *kisses* LOT *on the forehead as* CHICKEN *returns to the kitchen.*]

MYRTLE: Oh, child, you're hot as fire! They say feed a cold and starve a fever, but you got both.

LOT: I'm hungry for nothing.

MYRTLE: You're hungry for love, and you're gonna have supper with it.

LOT: At the same time, with no appetite for either?

MYRTLE: When the sun comes out like a bright new five dollar gold piece, your appetite for both will come out with it.

LOT: All of a sudden the days in this place are long and hot an' yellow and—time gets lost. . . . [*His eyes fall shut.*]

MYRTLE: I oughtn't to go down there after the way he mocked me but I smell fried potatoes which is something I cain't resist.

LOT: If you didn't smell fried potatoes you'd smell chicken. . . .

MYRTLE: What?

LOT: Nothing. Go down in your washable velvet and eat for us both.

MYRTLE: I want to say one thing more before I face that creature in the kitchen. You're precious to me, you're beautiful to me, I love you with all my heart, and if you don't feel good now, you're gonna feel wonderful later and you believe it. Believe it?

LOT [*with closed eyes and an enigmatic smile*]: Yes, I do, completely.

MYRTLE: You sure better. Here goes! —To what I don't know. . . .

[*She goes down the hall steps as if approaching a jungle.*]

MYRTLE [*entering the kitchen*]: Hi. —Hello.—How are you?

[*He ignores all three salutations.*]

Y'know what I thought I smelt down here?

CHICKEN: Me? Chicken?

MYRTLE: Ha, ha, no. I thought I smelt French fries down here.

CHICKEN: There's potatoes down here but there's nothing French about 'em.

MYRTLE: Bacon with 'em?

CHICKEN: You come down too late for the bacon.

MYRTLE: Oh, did I miss out on it?

CHICKEN: You sure missed out on the bacon but there's some bacon grease in the skillet with the potatoes.

MYRTLE: Bacon grease gives potatoes a wonderful flavor. [*She looks about nervously.*] —Memphis is famous for its French fries.

CHICKEN: 'Sthat what it's famous for?

MYRTLE: Yais. —I worked last winter at a place called the French Fried Heaven.

[CHICKEN *grunts at this information.*]

—Put on ten pounds. —The way they cooked French fries, they put the potatoes in a wire basket and put the wire basket in deep fat.

CHICKEN: The fried potatoes here come out of a skillet.

MYRTLE: Oh, I didn' expeck you t'have a wire basket here. —In the country. I'll, uh, help myself an' then take a plate up to Lot.

[*As she fills a plate with potatoes,* CHICKEN *turns the lamp up.*]

Where do you keep the silver?

CHICKEN: You mean knife an' fork?

MYRTLE: Just a fork. I don't need a knife for potatoes.

[CHICKEN *grunts.*]

Still hot.

CHICKEN: Who?

MYRTLE: I meant the potatoes.

CHICKEN: Aw. I misunnerstood you.

MYRTLE: —Here's the silver. It needs t'be polished. That colored girl Clara don't make herself very useful, I'll have to talk to her.

CHICKEN [*rising*]: Take this chair, this is a good chair for you.

MYRTLE: I don't want to take your chair. You stay where you are.

CHICKEN: No, you take this chair, I've warmed it up for you and I'm going back out for another look at the levee.

MYRTLE: Right away?

[*He is pulling on his hip boots.*]

CHICKEN: I'll stay a while if you want me in here with you.

MYRTLE: This is a perfeck time for us to get better acquainted, don't you think so?

[*She avoids his grinning look and sits gingerly down at the kitchen table.*]

CHICKEN: You don' have enough light.

MYRTLE: Yais, enough, I kin see.

CHICKEN [*pushing oil lamp toward her*]: Don't strain your eyesight an' go blind before time to.

MYRTLE [*noticing the knife with which he'd been carving something onto the table*]: —Is, uh, this, uh, this switch-blade knife your knife?

CHICKEN: —Is it your or Lot's knife?

MYRTLE: We don't, I don't, he don't—carry a switch-blade knife.

[*Tries to laugh; coughs.*]

CHICKEN: Then I reckon it'd be a safe bet that it's mine.

MYRTLE: Will you please put it away? I never could stand the sight of a big switch-blade knife like that fo' some—reason. . . .

CHICKEN: Why's that?

MYRTLE: —It, it— [*Shakes her head, tremulously.*] —Just, just—makes me uncomf'table always.

CHICKEN: —Reminds you of the end of one of the Mobile Hot Shots?

MYRTLE: —Yais. —No.

CHICKEN: Yais and no are two opposite answers. Maybe you mean maybe. [*He laughs and folds the switch-blade knife and puts it in his pocket.*]

MYRTLE: Maybe I ought to fill another plate fo' Lot an' eat with him upstairs. A sick person is lonesome.

CHICKEN: Eat a little with me befo' you go up. I need some company, too. [*He empties the rest of the potatoes in another plate and starts eating them.*]

MYRTLE [*in a strained voice*]: —I think I'll move this lamp a little your way.

[*She shoves it toward his seat at the table. He shoves it back toward hers.*]

A, uh, growin' boy or a—single, unmarried man, specially one in the country, allows his mind to dwell on an' give too much attention to—

CHICKEN: —To what? In your opinion?

MYRTLE: —You know what I'm talkin' about.

CHICKEN: I don't have no idea, not a bit.

MYRTLE: Well, I'll tell you, as if it was necessary. A single man in the country might amuse hisself by cutting a—indecent word and a indecent picture in a kitchen table.

CHICKEN: What brought that up, that subjeck?

MYRTLE: They's no point in me pretendin' I didn't notice these fresh wood-shavings on this table and what's been cut in the wood. I want to say just this. A thing like this's understandable in a, uh, growin' boy in the country but you're past that. You ought to be beyond that. An' you ought to know it's insulting to a clean-livin' woman who is not int'rested or attracted to—indecent things in her life.

CHICKEN: I'm glad you unnerstand that a single man in the country has got to amuse hisself.

MYRTLE: I said a growin' boy in the country, not a—adult—man with a—nawmul—mind.

CHICKEN: Aw. I misunnerstood you. You're not eatin' those good home-fried potatoes. You only like French-fried potatoes?

MYRTLE: —I've said what I hed t'say an' now, if you will excuse me, I'll take this plate up to Lot. [*She rises with plate.*]

CHICKEN: Lemme hold the lamp at the foot of the steps an' watch an' admire your hips as you climb up.

[*She hurries into the hall and he follows with the lamp. She stumbles on the steps and drops the plate.*]

Spilt 'em? On the steps?

MYRTLE: I could of got upstairs with them better without your— watching! Would you be good enough to put a, put some—

CHICKEN: If you mean more potatoes you're outa luck. They's nothin' but grease in th' skillet.

[*They face each other a silent moment. Then* CHICKEN *laughs and scrapes the spilt potatoes off the steps back onto the tin plate.*]

Here you are. He'll never know you spilt 'em unless you tell him—

MYRTLE: *I'd* know I spilt 'em an' wouldn't dream of—of not infawmin' my husban' exactly of all that wint on down here. Good night!

CHICKEN: Hurry back down agin, sister! Enjoyed your company down here! Hurry back down.

[*She stumbles rapidly up the steps with the tin plate. As she enters the bedroom,* CHICKEN *returns to the kitchen, sets the lamp down by carving and inscription and grins savagely at them. Then he blows out the lamp.*]

SCENE THREE

Immediately afterwards, upstairs. LOT *is in the chair, eyes shut.*

MYRTLE: Lot? Are you asleep?

LOT: No. No, I'm awake.

MYRTLE: Can you eat a little?

LOT: No. I don't want food.

MYRTLE: I got to tell you something. Something awful. I am still shaking all over. Feel how cold my hand is. Well. I come down in the kitchen. I said I smelled some bacon. He said I come down too slow. The bacon was gone. But I could have some potatoes. So I hed some potatoes. I had to swallow my pride because I was dyin' of hunger not having nothing to eat since that ham sandwich we hed on the road this mawnin. Well. I helped myself to potatoes and then I set down at the table. I started to try to make some polite conversation. Not that I wanted to talk to that son of a bitch but because I knowed that people living together under one roof have got to make some effort to get along. Well. I notice a pocket knife and some fresh wood shavings in the middle of the table. Well. That was peculiar but I said nothing about it. Then I noticed he kept turning the lamp up. Each time a little bit higher. Then all at once I noticed. I seen the reason. *That man is a lunatic!* You know what he had done? He had cut out a disgusting picture in the table, in the wood of the table, right in front of my plate, a disgusting word and a disgusting pitcher. I! —I started to choke! When I seen it. I sprung up from the table. He says, "What is the matter with you, Myrtle?" Just as innocent-like as you could imagine! Well. I didn't admit that I had seen a damn thing on that table. I just said, "I better take Lot up some food."

LOT [*mysteriously smiling*]: What was the picture of? A man or a woman?

MYRTLE: Both!

LOT: Both?

MYRTLE: Yes, both.

LOT: Doing what?

MYRTLE: Can't you imagine what? With his dirty mind?

[LOT *laughs and coughs.*]

You think it's funny?

LOT: I think everything's funny. In this world. I even think it's funny I'm going to die.

MYRTLE: It may surprise you a little but I'm going to tell you what *I* am planning to do. I'm planning to get on the phone and call to THE POlice.

LOT: How are you going to do that?

MYRTLE: He's got into his hip boots. He's going back out on that levee and soon as he goes I'm going to call the police.

LOT: You think they'll come.

MYRTLE: I reckon they will when I tell them he's out of his mind and I am your wife and afraid to stay in the house with him over this night!

LOT: Nobody will come. Nobody will answer the phone.

MYRTLE: Why do you say they won't come?

LOT: Have you forgotten this county is half under water, and the crest of the flood is still coming?

MYRTLE: I keep forgetting that fact because it's like a bad dream I don't believe. And anyhow. Decent people have got to be protected, flood or no flood, yes, come hell or high water.

LOT: —There he goes.

MYRTLE: Who? Chicken?

LOT: Who else is here but you and me and Chicken?

MYRTLE: Well! I'm going down there and try to phone the police.

LOT: See if you can get hold of his wallet.

MYRTLE: What for?

LOT: He's got a paper in it he made me sign. It leaves the place to him if I should die.

MYRTLE: And me? What about me! Left with nothing?

LOT: I don't know if the paper will still be good or not good if I die with a widow.

MYRTLE: —How could I git this paper?

LOT: How well can you hold liquor?

MYRTLE: I guess that question has a point but I don't see it.

LOT: I wondered if you could drink with a man till he passes out but you don't. Chicken's been drinking down there. I've heard him clump the liquor jug on the kitchen table every few minutes or so since we came upstairs, and he was probably drinking a good while before we got here.

MYRTLE: I guess you're drivin' at something but I don't know what.

LOT: Chicken always has on him, in his wallet, that legal paper that leaves this place to him when I go.

MYRTLE: I don't understand what—

LOT: Let me tell you this without interruption, Myrtle, and try to listen to me. Get Chicken drunk but don't get drunk yourself and when he passes out, get this legal paper out of his wallet, tear it to bits and pieces and burn 'em up. Then, as my wife, when I die, this place will be yours, go to you.— Valuable property.

MYRTLE: I don't know how to pretend to not drink but—

LOT: This paper in Lot's wallet—he sleeps on a cot in the kitchen—he keeps this wallet containin' this paper under his pillow like it was sacred to him. Which it is. Sacred. Is my head too vague to explain this?

MYRTLE: You've explained it, but it sounds like a risky suggestion, he's such a bull of a man, and—

LOT: Don't you want this place, all your own, when I go?

MYRTLE: Risky. Suppose he—?

LOT: Anything worth having and doing in this world is risky. So go down and use your charms on him and drink but out of your drink take little sips like a bird while he sloshes down his till he falls on his cot, passed out, and you take out his wallet and out of his wallet take that legal paper and destroy it. Own this place. It would haunt me in my grave and my mother in hers if this place went to Chicken. That paper gone, you'll own a good piece of property and you can run him off it, marry again, and be happy.

MYRTLE: How do I know if— ?

LOT: Here's your chance to own something.

MYRTLE: —Is this the reason you married me, baby, an' brought me down here?

LOT: I married and brought you down here to own a place of your own an' be a lady.

MYRTLE: —Well—I'll give it a try. Hmmm. I wasn't called the Petite Personality Kid for nothing.

LOT: Hear him? Coming back in the kitchen?

MYRTLE: Yais, down I go, wish me luck. God knows I'm gonna need it.

LOT: I wish you luck and my mother does, too.

[MYRTLE *picks up the oil lamp and starts to the door.*]

Do you have to remove the lamp and leave me gasping in dark?

MYRTLE: Don't I have to light myself down the stairs?

LOT: Go ahead, take it. The moon's out like the bleary eye of a drunkard.

MYRTLE: 'Sthere anything I can do for you 'fore I go down?

LOT: Nothing. Go down. Get the paper.

[*She exits from the bedroom with the lamp. The bedroom is completely dimmed out except for a faint and fitful streak of moonlight on* LOT *in the rocker.*]

SCENE FOUR

Immediately following, MYRTLE *descends the stairs with the lamp and the laundry. Hearing her,* CHICKEN *returns to the kitchen table and turns up the lamp.*

MYRTLE: —I thought you'd gone out of the house.

CHICKEN: —What would I go out for? That wet electric equipment that's gonna git wetter?

MYRTLE: —I'm afraid I let my nerves get the better of me. Let's forget it. I, uh, come down to tell you I'm worried sick about Lot. He has trouble drawing his breath.

CHICKEN: It's hard to draw breath without lungs.

MYRTLE: He won't stop smoking. And says it's the end of the world. I simply couldn't stand it a minute longer without a—drink. Have you got some liquor down here?

CHICKEN: They don't sell me bottle liquor in this county but I can git it by the jug from a—ole colored man that brews a pretty good brew.

MYRTLE: Is, uh, that the jug there?

CHICKEN: Yep, and it ain't drained yet. I'll give you a drink. —I treat you pretty nice, don't I? For a single man in the country?

MYRTLE: We just—haven't yet got used to each other. And this has been a day an' a night that would make any girl nervous with or without nerves in her.

CHICKEN: I guess you want a stiff drink, a pretty stiff one.

MYRTLE: Oh, uh, for me, just average. You have one with me, let's drink together an' git better acquainted. —Oh. This wash. I noticed you have a clothes line in the kitchen. Do you object if I hang up my undies to dry?

CHICKEN: Hang 'em up. [*She daintily hangs up some rayon panties and a brassiere.*] They'll dry out good in the flood.

MYRTLE: Do me a favor and stop reminding me of this—possible flood.

CHICKEN: It's not a possible flood, this flood is certain.

MYRTLE: Let's not—talk about it. I like drinking from a tin cup, I like the metal taste you git from it.

CHICKEN: —Why do you make that whistling noise when you breathe?

MYRTLE: I am choked up with asthma.

CHICKEN: Aw, you got as'ma.

MYRTLE: Oh, no, I haven't got asthma, it's got me. I got that allergy thing. You know about it—I wint to a Memphis doctor who give me the allergy tests and guess what he found out, he found out I was living with a cat and had a allergy to it. Yes, I had a cat I was real, real fond of, cat named Fluffy. Well, they discovered this cat, she had a allergy to me. I had to git rid of Fluffy, it was her or me. First I give her a great big head of a catfish, which was her favorite food. Like the last supper of the condemned. Then chloroformed her. Poor Fluffy. I was so attached to her and her to me.—I wept a bucket full of tears that night! Whew. [*rises*] From the way I suffer from my asthma tonight, I'm willing to bet that there's a cat somewhere on this place.

CHICKEN: I got a cat.

MYRTLE: That explains it.

CHICKEN: I brought her in for company tonight.

[*Lifts a cat in his lap.* MYRTLE *knew the cat was there but pretends to be surprised.*]

MYRTLE: Oh, no wonder I am choking with asthma, git that cat out of here, for heaven's sake, please!

CHICKEN: *Here, Kitty.* [*He lazily seizes cat and pulls up a trap door near the kitchen table and drops cat through it. She drops with a howl and a splash below. He drops the trap door shut.*]

MYRTLE: Why, that cellar is flooded! I heard a splash!

CHICKEN: You said you wanted her out.

MYRTLE: Out the door, not *drowned!*

[*She raises trap door and cries "Kitty!" He nudges her stooping figure with his knee. She screams and rolls on the floor.*]

Oh, my God, you tried to push me in! You tried to drown me!

CHICKEN: Ha ha ha!

MYRTLE: Oh, my God, my God, you tried to drown me!

CHICKEN: Ha ha ha ha ha ha ha!

LOT [*calling weakly above*]: *Myrtle, Myrtle!*

CHICKEN: Your lover is calling for you.

MYRTLE [crawling away on the floor]: Close! —Close that trap door!

CHICKEN: Aw, come on, knock it off! Nobody's going to drown you— Myrtle Turtle!

MYRTLE: You wanted to drown me like you drowned that cat!

CHICKEN: That cat ain't drowned. She swum on top of the wood-pile.—Same as you'd do if I put you down there with her.

MYRTLE: —I—cain't—swim!

CHICKEN: —Can you do anything? —Outside of bed?

MYRTLE: Chicken, please shut that trap door.

[*He kicks it shut.*]

Oh, my heart! How you scared me! [*Gasps and rises weakly.*]

Please, I—give me a shot of that—whiskey. . . .

CHICKEN: Go on. Pour you' self one.

MYRTLE [*breathlessly laughing*]: I'm afraid to git up! I swear to goodness I am!

CHICKEN: Aw, now, knock it off. I was just fooling a little.

MYRTLE [*cautiously crossing to table*]: Where is—where is a cup. My heart is—still beating!

CHICKEN: Shit, if your heart wasn' beatin' you'd be daid!

MYRTLE: Not like this! It's beatin' like a hammer!

CHICKEN: You remember that song?

MYRTLE [*nervously*]: Which—which song?

CHICKEN: "My heart beat like a ham-mer!
Your arms—wound around me tight!
And stars—fell on Alabama—last—night!"

MYRTLE: Yes, I do, I remember.—Do you remember this one? This one's another old-timer!

"Is it true what they say about Dixie?
Is a dream by that stream so sublime?

Do they laugh, do they love
Like they say in ev'ry song!
—If it's true—that's where *I—be—long!*"

CHICKEN: Ha ha ha ha ha! That one goes back a long way. Yes, siree, Bob, that's a real old-timer!

MYRTLE: And how about this one? Oh, this one is a—

LOT: Myr-*tlllllle!*

MYRTLE: Coming, honey, coming in just a minute!— [*Fearfully as he approaches the table toward her.*]

—Oh, this is fun, this—*singing*—I—love a song-fest, I love a—community—singing! Almost more than anything I can think of.

CHICKEN: Go on and sing! What song?

MYRTLE: —Wait till I—get my drink down! [*She walks in back of table with her whiskey in a tin cup.*]

CHICKEN: Wettin' your whistle, first?

MYRTLE: That's right, wetting my whistle!

CHICKEN: You almost wet something else when I pushed you toward that trap door! Huh, Myrtle?—*Ha ha ha ha ha!*

MYRTLE [*faintly and mirthlessly*]: Ha ha ha . . .

CHICKEN: Awright, now, what song was you going to sing for me, next on the program of old-time fav'rites?

MYRTLE: I wish that I had my little ukelele! My—dear ole uke!

CHICKEN: How 'bout a guitar, will that do?

MYRTLE [*with air of delight*]: Oh, hev you got a guitar!

CHICKEN: Yeah. Here. [*Removes guitar from back of closet door and hands it to her.*]

MYRTLE: This is a *man*size instrument!

CHICKEN: Don't you like a man-size instrument?

MYRTLE: I'm just wondering if I—

CHICKEN: Oh, I bet you can play it!

MYRTLE: We'll find out if I can.

CHICKEN: Sure you can. What's the number? I'll sing along with you!

MYRTLE: I love the old-time numbers. Don't you love them?

CHICKEN: The old-time tunes are the best.

MYRTLE: Here's one I can pick out with a—few—chords. . . . [*She is almost too breathless to sing.*]

"They's a long, long trail a-windin'
Into the land of my dreams!
Where the nightingale is— "

[*He moves toward the trap door. Her voice dies out in panic.*]

CHICKEN: Whacha stop for?

MYRTLE: You was going to sing with me.

CHICKEN: Sing it through once by you'self so I'll get the words.

MYRTLE: You mean you don't know the words to that old number? I thought everyone does. That song dates back a long ways, it dates back to World War One.

CHICKEN: Then how come you know it? You don't date back that far.

MYRTLE: It's one of those songs that—

CHICKEN: What?

MYRTLE: Never go out of—fashion. —Do me a favor, Chicken. Don't stand there by that trap-door to the cellar. It makes me too nervous to sing. Sit over here by me.

CHICKEN: Aw, you ain't nervous, you just think you're nervous.

MYRTLE: I'm nervous enough to scream.

CHICKEN: Don't scream. Sing! Sing some other old song.

MYRTLE: Like, uh—what?

CHICKEN: How about something religious?

MYRTLE: You really want something religious?

CHICKEN: Yeah, yeah, something from church, something out of the Hymn-book.

MYRTLE: Funny I—know lots of church songs but—can't think of any right now, ha ha! Ain't that funny? Wait a minute! Wait a minute! One's comin' back to me now. Oh, yes. Oh, yes, I got one, ha ha, I got one now! [*Assumes a rapt, grotesquely stiff smile, throws her head back and croons with her eyes half closed.*]

"My feet took a walk in heavenly grass.
All day while the sky shone clear as glass.
My feet took a walk in heavenly grass,
All night while the lonesome stars rolled past.
Then my feet come down to walk on earth,
And my mother cried when she give me birth.
Now my feet walk far and my feet walk fast,
But they still got an itch for heavenly grass.
But they still got an itch for heavenly grass."

CHICKEN: You're gettin' hoarse, Myrtle.

MYRTLE: I thought you was gonna sing with me.

CHICKEN: I don't sing good enough to.

MYRTLE: You got a *good* voice. You know, you always expect a big man is going to sing baritone or bass but they usually sing tenor? You got a sweet tenor voice. Ain't I silly? Gaspin' for breath like this!

CHICKEN: It's that cat allergy thing, you got that allergy thing!

MYRTLE: No, no, it's not cats, it's— !

CHICKEN: It's what? What, Myrtle?

MYRTLE: *Nerves!* A nervous condition!

CHICKEN: You're worried about that cat, that's what's your trouble. I think you're a member of that society, that human humane society, maybe the president of it [*He is pulling on his rubber hip boots.*]

MYRTLE: What's you getting into those rubber boots for?

CHICKEN: I'm going down in the basement to fetch that cat.

MYRTLE: Oh, she's done for, she's gone, now.

CHICKEN: No, she ain't. Come on, let's find that cat. You're worried about her, so let's go down in the basement an' find that cat.

MYRTLE [*backing away from him*]: You—*you* do that—if it's possible for you to do.

[*He jerks the trap door open.* MYRTLE *screams and hurls the guitar away as she rushes into the hall and scrambles up the stairs, screaming repeatedly.* CHICKEN *howls with laughter; then leaps abruptly into the basement with a splash, calling "pussy, pussy, pussy?" The cat yowls and* CHICKEN *laughs. He leaps back up from the trap door, still laughing, with the cat in his hand. He is still laughing and holding the cat as the stage dims out.*]

INTERMISSION.

SCENE FIVE

Immediately following. The bedroom is lighted and, at a much lower level, so are the back steps of the house where CHICKEN *sits with his cat. The parlor is now masked by an opaque transparency.* LOT *remains in the wicker chair in the bedroom. He is still smoking with his mother's ivory holder and wearing now her white silk wrapper. His "Mona Lisa" smile is more sardonic and the violet shadows about his eyes are deeper.* MYRTLE *stands, panting, in the doorway.*

LOT:—From the singing and other commotions I heard down there, I don't need to ask you if you got the paper. —Did you? No, you didn't.

MYRTLE: You listen here! Enough is enough and more than enough is too much!

LOT: You didn't get much liquor down him. —Did you?

MYRTLE: That man, that animal down there, could drink a liquor store dry and walk straight to another!

LOT: I thought you told me there wasn't a man on earth that you weren't able to manage. Well. If that statement was accurate, then either Chicken isn't a man or he isn't on earth. And I think he is both.

MYRTLE: Don't be sarcastic with *me*.

LOT: Don't shout so he can hear you. Can you speak without shouting?

MYRTLE: I said don't be sarcastic with me. I'm not in a mood to take it after what I went through in the kitchen with your so-called brother.

LOT: My opposite type. I hate that man with a passion.

MYRTLE: I'm terrified of him. Is there a key to this door to lock him out?

LOT: No. I hate and despise him with such a passion that if this place or anything on this place became his property—

MYRTLE: S'pose he comes up here and drags me down?

LOT: Neither mother or me could rest in peace in Old Gray Cemetery.

MYRTLE: I'm not in a cemetery. What about me?

LOT: What about you except you—

MYRTLE: There's not just you, there's me. The selfish streak in your nature is wide as the river—flooding!

LOT: Have you ever owned much of anything in your life?

MYRTLE: Yais! My self-respeck an' decency as a woman!

LOT: In addition to that, marvelous as it is, would you like to own and possess entirely as your own a place that's worth much more than it gives appearance of being?

MYRTLE:—Worth what? In cash?

LOT: Over fifty thousand and could increase well-managed. . . . [*Long pause*] —Well? Attractive to you or not?

MYRTLE: I've never owned a stone I could call my own.

LOT: —A pitiful confession, but now's your chance if you want it.

[*A pause as* MYRTLE *reflects.*]

MYRTLE: —Sugar? Baby? Why don't you get in bed instead of sitting at a window in a light silk wrapper?

LOT: I breathe better sitting up in a chair—and can look at the sky.

MYRTLE: The sky's clouded over.

LOT: Once in a while the moon comes out of those fast-moving clouds, and it—says things to me in the soft voice of my mother. . . .

MYRTLE: I wish you would get in bed and let me hold you and love you.

LOT: You don't have to hold me to love me.

MYRTLE: You're shivering. Lemme put something heavier around you like a blanket.

LOT: No, no, don't. I don't want to be smothered.

MYRTLE: Chicken's out of the kitchen, so I am going back in it and fill a hot-water bottle for you an' git you in this bed if you like it or not.

LOT: There's not any hot-water bottle.

MYRTLE: I never travel without one. It's in my traveling case.

LOT: I should've known.

MYRTLE: What?

LOT: —Nothing, and not much of that either.

MYRTLE: That seems to be what you know, but I am going back down there and get hold of that paper, how I don't know, but somehow. And I'm going down there in my show costume as the Personality Kid. [*She changes quickly into the costume.*]

LOT: I think what attracts you back down there is nothing made of rubber and nothing made of paper, whether you face it or not.

MYRTLE: Your fever's gone to your haid, if you think that.

LOT: I don't just think it, I know it. —I won't see daylight again.

MYRTLE: I can pick you up and carry you to the bed and that's what I'm gonna do when I've filled my hot-water bottle.

LOT: Anybody with arms could pick me up—if they wanted to force me against my will.

MYRTLE: Is it against your will to be loved and made well?

LOT: —No. —If you can't make him pass out to get that paper, knock him out with a hammer that's in the drawer of the kitchen table and don't come up here again without that paper. You get that paper and you can pick me up and carry me to the bed with no resistance and I'll—rest in your arms. . . .

MYRTLE: I got to take this lamp to get down the stairs in my —shaky condition.

LOT: Take it. I get enough light from the sky.

[*She goes back into the hall and starts down the steps. She is halfway down them with the lamp when* CHICKEN *slams open the back door and enters the lower hall.*]

MYRTLE [*terrified gasp*]: HAH! [*She drops the oil lamp on the stairs; it goes out.*]

CHICKEN: Trying to start a fire? Burn your place down? Before it goes under water?

MYRTLE: —I thought—

CHICKEN: Don't strain your brain thinkin'.

MYRTLE: Lot's—Lot's havin' a chill. Terrible. I want to fill up a hot-water bottle for him. Kin I come down?

CHICKEN: Why do you ask to come downstairs in your house?

MYRTLE: I don't possess this house or anything in it except what I brought here with me.

CHICKEN: All that electric equipment to make life easy for you?

[*He laughs and enters the kitchen.* MYRTLE *stops in the downstairs hall and speaks tremulously*—]

MYRTLE: Please do me a favor before I come in the kitchen.

CHICKEN: Such as what? [*He turns up the kitchen lamp.*]

MYRTLE: Of course I know you wuh teasing me with that trap door open, but would you please push the table over it now.

CHICKEN: It ain't open now.

MYRTLE: Open or shut, I couldn't be comf'table in the kitchen unless that table was over that trap-door.

CHICKEN: [*pushing the table with his foot*]: You're Mistress of the House, the Lady in it. Whatever you tell me to do I'm obliged t'do it.

[MYRTLE *moves nervously to the kitchen threshold.*]

MYRTLE: I'm just a visitor here, but would you push the table over the trap-door a little bit further than that? Please?

CHICKEN: Why, sure, Mrs. Lot Ravenstock. A hired hand on a place always does what pleases the lady and the boss-man. [*He shoves the table further with his foot.*]

—How's that now, does that suit you?

MYRTLE: [*entering the kitchen*]: Yes, thank you, fine, perfeck. I feel much more easy.

CHICKEN: You're a city lady and I'm a country boy with common habits. I hope you'll excuse me for them.

MYRTLE: I've been teased in my life. I had two older brothers, Jack and Jim, that teased me nearly to death. Y'see, my curls were long then. And they would pull them and yell "Ding-dong." Oh, it never hurt much but it always scared me. Holler? Oh, would I holler! Sometimes it wouldn't be necessary for them to pull my curls, they could just say "Ding-Dong" and I'd scream fit to kill and blaze a trail to the house, so you see I'm used to teasing, but so much has happened in the last few hours I feel un-strung. —A little.

CHICKEN: You're walking around like you wuh lookin' fo' something.

MYRTLE: A kettle to boil water in. So I can fill a hot-water bottle in my traveling case.

[*She removes the hot-water bottle from the beat-up case and wanders distractedly about the kitchen.*]

CHICKEN: Why don'tcha put the hot-water bottle down while you look for the kettle so you'll have both your hands free?

MYRTLE: Ha! —What's the matter with me? I sure don't seem to have my head on my—!

[CHICKEN *rises, setting the cat on the floor.*]

That cat didn't drown in the cellar?

CHICKEN: Shit, no. You can't drown a cat unless you put her in a sack full of rocks. She swum on top of th' woodpile. Didn't you, pussy? [*He hands a kettle to her.*]

MYRTLE: Thanks. [*She sets the kettle on the stove.*]

CHICKEN: —Is that how you do it?

MYRTLE: —Huh?

CHICKEN: —You git the kettle hot first and thin put th' water in it?

MYRTLE: Ha ha! Ain't that *somethin?* Shows how upset I am! I put that empty kettle on the stove without water in it!

CHICKEN: Gimme th' kettle. I'll git you some water in it from the rain barrel out there.

[*Crosses to the door with the kettle and descends to the rain barrel. She follows to the door.*]

MYRTLE: They say rain water's the purest water there is.

CHICKEN: Is that what they say? Well, nothin's too pure for Lot.

MYRTLE: —Not that it matters in a hot-water bottle. . . .

CHICKEN: Yeah, well . . .

[*Hands her the dripping kettle. She returns inside. He watches her back as she moves to the stove and gives a slight wolf whistle. She gets the kettle on the stove with a bang that makes her give a startled laugh.*]

What's the joke?

[*She goes on laughing, helplessly.*]

Let me in on the joke, it must be a good one.

MYRTLE: I just, just! *—got—hysterics!* [*Continues giggling.*]

CHICKEN: They's two ways to stop hysterics in a woman. One way is to give her a slap in the face and the other way is to lay her. Sometimes you got to do both.

MYRTLE: Oh, I'm all right now. I come out of hysterics as quick as I go in them. —How come a handsome young man like you is still single?

CHICKEN: —I'm dark-complected.

MYRTLE: What of it?

CHICKEN: They's not been a woman on this place, not since Miss Lottie died, but the colored girl Clara and she's took to the hills to get away from the flood.

MYRTLE: You mention this flood like it didn't scare you a bit.

CHICKEN: Floods make the land richer.

MYRTLE: What good does that do if you drown?

CHICKEN: I'm not gonna drown. —Are you?

MYRTLE: Lord God Jesus, I pray to my Saviour I won't!

CHICKEN: You'd do better praying to Chicken.

MYRTLE: I'm counting on your protection.

CHICKEN: You better not count on that.

MYRTLE: That's what I'm counting on, Chicken.

CHICKEN: Count on nothing. Set down.

MYRTLE: I prefer to stay on my feet a while if—

CHICKEN: If what?

MYRTLE: —If you don't object.

CHICKEN: Shit, I don't mind if you stand on your head if you want to! But look. I got this old auto cushion I'll put on this here chair and'll make you a nice soft seat. I know a woman don't like a hard seat, does she? Well, here's a real soft cushion for you to sit on while we talk.

MYRTLE: —Thanks! [*She seats herself tensely on the edge of the auto cushion.*]

CHICKEN [*with a slow, wolfish grin*]: Now you got *three* cushions?

MYRTLE: *—Three? —OH! —Ha ha!* —yaissss—three . . .

[*Loud silence in the kitchen.*]

CHICKEN: You feel comf'table?

MYRTLE: Yaiss! Yes, very! Are you?

CHICKEN: I always make myself comfortable as I can.

MYRTLE: Why not? You should! —a man should . . .

CHICKEN: —Should what?

MYRTLE: —Why—uh—make himself as comf'table as he—can . . .

CHICKEN: —How about you? Are you comf'table, too? On those three soft cushions?

MYRTLE: Yes, I told you I was. I'm just a little worried about my husband. I had no idea, I simply had no notion at all that he was in such a bad condition as this. I mean I . . . I just didn't have an idea . . .

CHICKEN: It's like you bought a used car that turned out to be a lemon.

MYRTLE: Oh, that's not how I look at it. That boy has touched the deepest chord in my nature. I mean I . . . [*She suddenly sobs.*]

CHICKEN: Quit that. I want to talk to you.

MYRTLE: Yes, talk!

CHICKEN: I guess you know the setup.

MYRTLE [*struggling for composure*]: The what?

CHICKEN: The setup. Do you know it?

MYRTLE [*with a weak attempt at levity*]: The only setup I know of is in a dry state they'll serve you a setup for liquor but not the liquor. You got to bring that with you.

CHICKEN: —If I was your lawyer I would advise you not to try to be funny.

MYRTLE: Can't we—joke a little?

CHICKEN: I'd advise you aginst it.

MYRTLE: Awright, I'll take that advice, but, Chicken, do you know that all the electric equipment I won as the Take-Life-Easy Queen is still in that car with a leakin' top bein' rained on?

CHICKEN: Fawgit that stuff. It can't be saved from floodwater. Can you concentrate on the legal setup if I explain it to you, or do you think it's something that don't concern you?

MYRTLE: I'm—anxious to know the—setup. Is the kettle boilin', is that water hot yet?

CHICKEN: Fawgit th' kettle. The fire is low in the stove.

MYRTLE: But I told Lot I'd—

CHICKEN: You don't seem t'want to know about the setup.

MYRTLE: Oh, that's not true, I do!

CHICKEN: I'll explain it to you.

MYRTLE: Yais, wonderful, do that! Whatever concerns this place an' my future life on it is impawtent t' me to understand an' t'know.

CHICKEN: Lot an' me are half brothers. Has that sunk into your haid yet?

MYRTLE: Oh, yes, that I do know. It come out in the, the—conversation we hed when we—first met, this—day.

CHICKEN: That's right. You got that straight. Maybe you know the rest of it.

MYRTLE: Lemme pour you some liquor while you explain the setup.

[*She tries to lift the jug off the table but her hands are too weak and shaky.*]

CHICKEN: Cain't lift the jug, you're so nervous about the set-up. Open your mouth and I'll pour some liquor down *you.*

MYRTLE: Thanks, I thank you. I couldn't git through this night without liquor in me. Could you?

CHICKEN: Mouth open.

[*She opens her mouth a little: He presses the mouth of the jug to it. The liquor runs down her chin and neck.*]

MYRTLE: Oh, it's stainin' my dress!

CHICKEN: You wouldn't swallow the liquor, drooled it out.

MYRTLE: I wasn't actually thirsty. You drink some. I like to see a man drink.

CHICKEN: What I am going to do is tell you about the setup, all of it. The rest that you might now know.

MYRTLE: What is the rest of the setup?

CHICKEN: Daddy got Lot in marriage but not me. You're lookin' at what is called a wood's-colt. [*He perches himself on the table and the light is hot on him.*] Whin I was ten years old he married this little blond haided woman that worked in a beauty shop in Clarksdale. Are you list'nin' or still too nervous to lissen?

MYRTLE: I'm list'nin' close. All ears.

CHICKEN: I wouldn't say that about you but I'd advise you to lissen close as you're able to me. This little lady that worked in the beauty parlor in Clarksdale was named Miss Lottie, so when

Lot was bawn, he got the name of Lot. Legal; bawn in marriage. Not a wood's-colt. Me—wood's-colt. You know what a wood's-colt is?

MYRTLE: No, I don't know that I know. All I know is you look—

CHICKEN: —Dark-complected?

MYRTLE: Foreign. —Foreign?

CHICKEN: My son of a bitch of a daddy got me offen a dark-complected woman he lived with in Alabama. —What about it?

MYRTLE: Why—nothing!

[*Slight pause.*]

Ain't you drinkin' no more? This awful night?

CHICKEN: Why're you so anxious for me to drink more?

MYRTLE: I don't like drinking alone. It makes me lonesome.

CHICKEN: I can drink you under this kitchen table, tonight.

MYRTLE: I'd rather stay on my feet with the flood you say's coming.

CHICKEN: You'd rather drown standing up?

MYRTLE: Don't talk about drowning. You wouldn't let that happen.

CHICKEN: —Let's get back to the setup. —Lot's mother, Miss Lottie, she thought she was surely going to bury my daddy. Hell, he was sixty when he married Miss Lottie.

MYRTLE: Is that what you mean by the setup?

CHICKEN: Just shut up and listen. —She'd no sooner got married to him that she begun to cheat on him with a good-looking young Greek fellow that had a fruit store in town. Why, ev'ry afternoon, Miss Lottie would say to daddy, "Daddy, I think I will drive in town to buy some fruit to make us a nice fruit salad." And when she got to the store, the store man would let her in and lock the door and she'd stay in for two hours and come out with four or five peaches like it had took her them two hours to pick out that small bag of peaches.

MYRTLE: Why didn't you tell your daddy?

CHICKEN: If I had told him, he'd've told her I told him, and she would of got me thrown outa here in minutes! —Well, she did bury my daddy and the place was hers but she didn't have long to hold it. The Greek sold out his fruit store, quit Miss Lottie, and left. —He just left town but Miss Lottie left the world.

MYRTLE: Daid. Yes. Lot told me. —Tragic.

CHICKEN: Well, she lived long enough to throw me off the place. Called me in her little parlor one day and fired me like a field hand. "Chicken," she said, "I think it's just about time for you to clear off this place and make your own way in the world." I said, "Well, gimme what's comin' to me." —What she give me amounted to just about the pay that a field hand gets for a week's work. It got me down the state to Meridian where I worked in a sawmill till. . . . And then this happened—Miss Lottie couldn't go on without trips to that fruit store so she quit eating, quit sleeping—quit breathing. And one month after she died, Lot started dying. One lung gone and one going, but trying to run this place. Didn't take long for him to find out he couldn't, so I begun to hear from him. He sent for me to come back and operate this place for him, sent for me twice by letter and a third time by wire. First and only wire *I* ever got in my life. Chicken, come back, was the message, I will make a deal with you. —Well, I'm no fool.

MYRTLE: No, no, you're no fool.

CHICKEN: I said, "All right, but I'm going to name the deal, and here's the deal." I said, "If you want me to run this place for you, well, here's the deal. Whin you are through with TB! —it goes to me. . . ."

MYRTLE: TB?

CHICKEN: You ain't paying attention to what I tell you. Not TB. The place, this *place!*

MYRTLE: —Oh! —So that's the setup.

CHICKEN: Yes, Ma'am, that is the setup.

MYRTLE: Oh. Uh-huh. I see. . . .

CHICKEN: You don't look happy about it!

MYRTLE: Don't I? Well, now, after all, you can't expect me to be overjoyed about it. I mean, after all, I'm human. And—

CHICKEN: And what?

MYRTLE: —Nothin, nothin but—

CHICKEN: But what?

MYRTLE: —If Lot dies I'm his widow and—

CHICKEN: That's just exactly the point that I'm coming to later, that's just the little situation we're tryin to git straightened out right now in this kitchen before the floodwater comes. I got a decision to make.

MYRTLE: What decision?

CHICKEN: A big one. A big one for you and me both. —Have you ever climbed on a roof?

MYRTLE: Me? Climbed on a roof? No. Not that I can remember. It don't seem—likely. . . . Why? Why do you ask me if I ever climbed on a roof?

CHICKEN: If you can't climb on a roof Lot won't have a widow when the floodwater comes. Now do you understand why I asked you that question? —Yeah. I can see that you do. So now to go on with what— What's the matt— ? Why are you getting up?

[MYRTLE *has risen stiffly from the chair with a look of slow and dreadful comprehension. Her breathing is audible and rapid.*]

—Your breath is whistling again. You want the cat out of here?

MYRTLE: *No, no, no, no, no, no, no!*

CHICKEN: I can put her back in the cellar if she is giving you as'ma.

MYRTLE: No, no, no, I'm all right, I'm—*fine*, I'm—all right. . . .

CHICKEN: Then why don't you stay in your seat? Ain't that auto cushion comfortable to sit on?

MYRTLE: Sure, it's—fine!

[*She remains standing, her eyes wide and bright but not focussed. He rises deliberately and picks up the auto cushion, examines it and dusts it and puts it back down again.*]

CHICKEN: You women have got a lot of heat in you. That cushion is warm from your body. Why don't you sit down while I finish explaining the setup?

MYRTLE: Oh, it's all clear now. I understand the setup and I want you to know, here is my right hand to God, that everything you told me is okay as far as I am concerned. I got no designs on nothing. You know it's funny how quickly the human mind changes! Ain't it queer how quick it changes? I had my heart set on a quiet, happy married life. Now what I want most in the world is to return to show business! —that's what I'm going to do, I'm going to cut out all fats and sweets and fried foods and get back my shape and go straight back to show business. It keeps you alive. It keeps you trim. It keeps you alert. It's the business for me. Absolutely no other can compare with it for keeping you healthy and active. —Now I think I can fill that hot-water bottle and take it up to that poor child I married . . . —*God please pity us both!*

[*She starts toward the stove but he seizes her wrist.*]

CHICKEN: I want you to stay sitting here till I've finished talking to you. You going to do that?

MYRTLE: —Why—sure!

CHICKEN: Good. Take a shot of this liquor. It might be good for your as'ma.

MYRTLE: Why, thanks! [*The tin cup shakes: She lifts it with both hands to her lips.*] —thanks. . . .

CHICKEN: So I said to him. I said to my half brother, "Lot, I want this place when you're gone. I been on this place all my life and I want to stay on this place all my life till I die. I was here before you come to it and I want to be here when you go. Is that understood? Is that understood, now, clearly?"

MYRTLE: Yes, yes, clearly, clearly . . .

CHICKEN: Good. So the place goes to Chicken, the place and everything on it goes to Chicken when you die.

MYRTLE: *Me? Die?*

CHICKEN: *Lot!*

MYRTLE: —Oh . . .

CHICKEN: Yes! "OH!"—we got to get things straightened out. . . .

MYRTLE: I told you I—

CHICKEN: Has anyone ever told you you talk too much? If I had married a woman with such a loose mouth, I'd put a stopper in it. "All right," I said. "All right. That's the agreement and I want it on paper, so let's put it on paper. Otherwise I don't stay." He said, "Stay, stay, we'll put it on paper," so we put it on paper. Had it drawn up, legal. Notary seal. Witnesses' names put on it. Signed in their presence! Now! [*Removes wallet and unfolds from about it a thick rubber band.*] I got this paper to prove it. The paper we drawn up between us with a notary seal and names of witnesses on it.

[*She stretches out her hand as he produces the paper from his wallet.*]

Oh, no. Someone's got itchy fingers. —Look but don't touch! —Understand? I never let this paper out of my hands. I sleep with this paper underneath my pillow and when I wake up in the mawning, you know what I find? I find my hand clutching my wallet with this paper in it. Even in my sleep I protect this paper! I guard it with my life and my soul and my body. Because it gives me this place when my half brother is gone! So now you see.

MYRTLE: Oh, yes, now I see.

CHICKEN: You ain't even looking at it. Look at this paper, will you? [*He shakes it in front of her.*] Does it look legal to you? You see this notary seal and names of witnesses on it? You see Lot's signature on it and my signature on it?

MYRTLE: Yes, yes!

CHICKEN: You want more light so you can see it more clearly? [*He turns up the lamp.*] There now, you can see it clearly!

MYRTLE: —It, it—sure looks—legal.

CHICKEN: —Yeah, but—you never can tell. . . .

MYRTLE: —What?

CHICKEN: A smart Jew lawyer might find some loopholes in it or make some if some wasn't there! —'specially if there was a widow surviving. . . . —I guess you think that I'm hard. Well, I got to be hard. A man and his life both got to be equally hard. Made out of the same hard thing. Man, rock. Life, rock. Otherwise one will break and the one that breaks won't be life. The one that breaks is the soft one and that's never life. If one is the soft one, the soft one that breaks will be man, not life, no, no, not life! —that's rock . . . yep—rock! Solid rock. . . . —Now then if you're satisfied that this is a legal paper I'll put it away.

MYRTLE: Of course I can see it is legal.

CHICKEN: But law is tricky. I never figured that Lot was going to git married. I certainly never thought he'd leave a widow. So I am faced with this important decision. Whether or not to haul you up on the roof when the house is flooded. Because if I do, then Lot will have a widow and this thing here might not be worth the paper it's typewritten on. You see what I mean about it? You see why I got to think this whole thing out step by step as careful as possible, do you? —Naw, I never thought he would leave a widow. You see? You see how easy it is to git buggered up? Law is a tricky thing. I never would of dreamed that son of a bitch would marry and leave a widow. And maybe now that changes the situation. Maybe now this agreement will not hold up in a court of law.

MYRTLE: I wouldn't—worry about it.

CHICKEN: Naw, you wouldn't worry about it. Why would you worry about it? You'd git the place, not Chicken!

MYRTLE: I, I, I —don't want this place! What would I do with this place?

CHICKEN: Want it or not you'd git it if bein his widow makes this paper—

MYRTLE [*rising stiffly*]: Look, Chicken!

CHICKEN: —makes this paper not good!

MYRTLE: Chicken, Chicken, look here!

CHICKEN: That's what he figured. Son of a bitch thought he'd screw me by leaving a widow. But one thing he didn't count on was the house being flooded and him and his widow both—

MYRTLE: Oh, now, look here, Chicken!

CHICKEN: Him and his widow both!

MYRTLE: Chicken!

CHICKEN: —drowned in it!—unless I haul his widow up on the roof.

MYRTLE: *Chicken, I—can't catch my breath!* I got a bad asthma attack, it's that—

CHICKEN: Huh?

MYRTLE [*gasping*]: Allergy thing, that—

CHICKEN: You want the cat out of here?

MYRTLE: Not, not, not in the—cellar but—

CHICKEN: Come on, pussy. You go set in the parlor.

[*He lifts the cat and crosses into the hall with her, shoves her into the parlor and kicks the door shut.* MYRTLE *stands gasping like a fish out of water, leaning for support against table.*]

MYRTLE: Chicken, this, this, this joke is gone on too long. I, I. We, we.

CHICKEN: Take a good breath. Then talk.

MYRTLE: I'm trying to catch one! —Lot an' me, we—ain't—married!

CHICKEN: You an Lot ain't married?

MYRTLE: No, a-course not! Are you kiddin? [*She tries to laugh.*] You didn't *believe* that, did you? Ha ha! I'm surprised at you for being so, so—gullible! Ha ha!—ha—ha . . . —Why, me and that boy are no more married than the man in the moon!

CHICKEN: He showed me a license.

MYRTLE: Yeah, but you said yourself you can buy those things for two bits at a novelty store to git you a hotel room to lay a woman!

CHICKEN: And the "Just Married" sign and the old shoes tied to the car?

MYRTLE: A joke, can't you take a joke? Ha ha!

CHICKEN: This is no jokin' matter.

MYRTLE: Well, it was just a joke, Chicken, it was all just a joke, Ha ha!

[*Her laugh is hollow: it expires in a gasp.*]

CHICKEN: Yeah. Well. *Maybe.*

MYRTLE: They's no maybe about it. I ought to know I'm not married!

CHICKEN: No?

MYRTLE: No! Look, whin I take that step, a step as serious in my life as marriage would be, I wouldn't take it with a—TB case! You want to know something? You want to know something, Chicken?

CHICKEN: Yeah, I want to know something.

MYRTLE: That poor boy bleaches his hair, not only has TB but bleaches his hair. Look, now, seriously! Do you imagine that I'd give up a career in show business to marry a, a, to marry a, to, to, to marry a—

CHICKEN: —What's wrong now?

MYRTLE [*with a grimace*]: Throat's! Stopped!

CHICKEN: Choked on lies!

MYRTLE: No! No!

CHICKEN: That's what you done, you choked you'self on lies!

MYRTLE: Now, Chicken.

CHICKEN: "Now, Chicken."

MYRTLE: Oh, don't mock me, please!

CHICKEN: I think I better take a new look at that paper. Go up and git me that paper.

MYRTLE: Which, which paper?

CHICKEN: This license you say you got from a novelty store.

MYRTLE: Lot's, Lot's got it, he's got it! I, I don't have it, Lot's got it!

CHICKEN: Jesus. I never seen anybody in such a condition as you seem to be in.

MYRTLE: I told you about how scared I am of— [*She turns away, gasping as if drowning.*] —water! [*Gasps twice and clutches chair back.*] —Ever since I was baptized by a preacher that held me under—too *long*. . . .

CHICKEN: I'm not going to hold you under. Shit. It wouldn't be necessary to hold you under. If you can't climb on the roof when the house is flooded, and I don't reckon you can. It wouldn't be necessary to hold you under. Unless you float like a cork. Do you float like a cork?

MYRTLE: Oh, God, Chicken, why don't you take my word? I'm not Lot's widow, I mean I won't be his widow if he dies, cause we ain't married.

CHICKEN: Go up an git that paper.

MYRTLE: —Whin?

CHICKEN: Now.

MYRTLE: Wait till I catch my breath.

CHICKEN: Git the paper now and catch your breath later.

MYRTLE: I can't climb stairs without breath. And Lot's water's boiling, the kettle is boiling, I'll fill his hot-water bottle.

CHICKEN: All right. Fill his hot-water bottle and git that paper and bring it down here so I can give it a careful examination.

MYRTLE: Help me. I can't— do —this!

[*She drops the hot-water bottle.* CHICKEN *picks it up and fills it by the stove.*]

CHICKEN: Now go up and give him his hot-water bottle and git that marriage license while you're up there.

[*She starts upstairs.*]

CHICKEN [*to her back*]: Hurry.

MYRTLE: I'm goin' fast as I can, unable to breathe!

CHICKEN: You're breathin'.

[*She opens the bedroom door and calls softly.*]

MYRTLE: Lot? Lot, baby? Are you asleep, Lot, baby?

[*Light falls on him: He looks like a Far Eastern idol. He doesn't answer except by rocking his wicker chair in the pool of moonlight.*]

How are you, now, Lot, baby?

LOT: You know how I am: still breathing. Have you got Chicken drunk yet?

MYRTLE: I don't think he's gonna get drunk, liquor don't seem to affect him.

LOT: Then you won't get the paper and he'll get the place.

MYRTLE: —Well . . .

LOT: You sound resigned to it, Myrtle.

MYRTLE: —If this house is flooded, both floors, could *you* get me up on the roof?

LOT: Aw. Chicken has offered to get you up on the roof.

MYRTLE: You brought me here and put me at his mercy, don't forget that.

LOT: I thought you could handle Chicken.

MYRTLE: You gave me no warning.

CHICKEN [*impatiently, below stairs*]: *Hey! Come on!*

LOT: What's he want? Just your company down there?

MYRTLE: I got your hot-water bottle. Here's your hot-water bottle.

LOT: My chill's gone now. I'm burning up with fever. What I need's an ice pack.

MYRTLE: Honey, you know there ain't no ice in this house.

LOT: What were you doing down there with Chicken?

MYRTLE: I was waitin' for the kettle to boil so I could fill up this hot-water bottle which you don't want no more.

LOT: You know something?

MYRTLE: Huh?

LOT: I think you're a whore.

MYRTLE [*sadly, almost gently*]: Lot, baby, that is the most cruel thing that anybody has ever said to me in my entire life. Here is my right hand to God! After all that I have suffered to stay on the straight and narrow, to be called a whore by my just married husband.

LOT: I said it looks like I married a prostitute and brought her home for Chicken.

MYRTLE: I know, I know what you said, you don't have to repeat it. The strange thing about this is, *I*, I haven't blamed *you! You* are blaming *me!*

[*Dialogue overlaps.*]

LOT: I married a whore and . . .

MYRTLE: Here I'm standing, here, full of TB germs because you . . .

LOT: . . . brought her back here to Chicken.

MYRTLE: . . . lied! Lied to me! And have bleached hair and—

LOT: Goddam whore an' brought her back here to Chicken for him to lay while I die up here in this rocker, you *common*-trash!

MYRTLE: God! —How mean people are! —I'm going downstairs after that.

LOT: Sure, and it makes how many times you gone down them!? To Chicken?

MYRTLE: This time is the last time. I'm not going to come back up. Not till you call me up and apologize to me and maybe not even then. No, not even then—maybe. . . .

[*Starts out: Turns back and roots in his coat pocket: coat hangs on hook on wall.*]

LOT: What are you doing? What did you take from my coat?

MYRTLE: Our marriage license! Your half brother wants to look at it to see if it's real.

[*She starts out again:* LOT *begins to laugh softly as she closes the door. She pushes it open again and says—*]

—What are you laughing at?

LOT: At life! —I think it's funny.

MYRTLE: —I think it's like a bad dream. . . .

LOT: —A bad dream can be funny!

MYRTLE: —I guess it can. At that. . . . [*Closes door rather softly.* CHICKEN *waits in the hall. She descends.*]

SCENE SIX

[MYRTLE *enters kitchen.*]

MYRTLE: Here it is, this is it. [*Hands him the license.*] You can see it's no good.

CHICKEN: —It's got signatures on it.

MYRTLE: Sure, they put signatures on 'em to make 'em look real, but—

CHICKEN: This looks like a genuine license to me.

MYRTLE: I give you my right hand to God! —That thing is fake!

CHICKEN: Don't give me your right hand to God. I don't want it and He don't want it neither. Nobody wants your right or left hand to nothing. However, I'll keep this thing. I'll put it with my legal agreement with Lot. [*He folds the license into his wallet and studies her somberly.*] Are you able to write?

MYRTLE: Why, uh—yais!

CHICKEN: I don't mean just your name.

MYRTLE: No! Yais, I mean yais! —I been through four grades of school.

CHICKEN: Take a seat at this table. I'm gonna give you a little test in writing. [*He tears a sheet from a writing tablet and sets it before her with a pen and an ink bottle.*] You say you are able to write, and I am able to read. You see this pin an' paper I set befo' you?

MYRTLE: Yais! Perfectly! Plainly!

CHICKEN: Do you write standing up?

MYRTLE: Yais! No, I mean no! [*She scrambles into the chair.*]

CHICKEN: Now take this pin and write out on this paper what I tell you to write.

MYRTLE: What do you—?

CHICKEN: Shut up. I'm gonna dictate to you a letter that you will write an' sign and this letter will be to me.

MYRTLE: Why should I write you a letter when, when—you're right here?

CHICKEN: You'll understand why when you write it and write it out plain enough so anybody can read it.

MYRTLE: —My hand is—

CHICKEN: What?

MYRTLE: Shakin'!

CHICKEN: Control it.

MYRTLE: It's hard to control it with my nerves so unstrung.

CHICKEN: Which hand do you write with, with the left or the right?

MYRTLE: Oh, with the right, I'm right-handed.

CHICKEN: Well, give me that shaky right hand.

MYRTLE: What do you want with my hand?

CHICKEN: Stop it shakin'. [*He takes hold of her hand in both of his.*]

MYRTLE: What big hands you got, Chicken.

CHICKEN: Feel the calluses on 'em? I got those calluses on my hands from a life of hard work on this fuckin' place, worked on it like a nigger and got nothin' for it but bed and board and the bed was a cot in the kitchen and the board was no better than slops in the trough of a sow. However, things do change, they do gradually change, you just got to wait and be patient till the time comes to strike and then strike hard. [*He is rubbing her hand between his.*] Now it's comin', that time. This place is gonna be mine when the house is flooded an' I won't be unhappy sittin' on the roof of it till the flood goes down.

MYRTLE: No. Me neither. I'll be—pleased and—relieved!

CHICKEN: You mean if you are still in the land of the livin'.

MYRTLE: Don't make my hand shake again.

CHICKEN: I guess you think that I'm hard.

MYRTLE: I don't think a man should be soft.

CHICKEN: You know what life is made out of?

MYRTLE: Evil, I think it's evil.

CHICKEN: I think that life just plain don't care for the weak. Or the soft. A man and his life. Like I said, a man and his life both got to be made out of the same stuff or one or the other will break and the one that breaks won't be life. Now then. Your hand ain't shakin.

MYRTLE: No. My hand has stopped shaking because . . .

CHICKEN: —What?

MYRTLE: I know in my heart that you don't hate Myrtle.

CHICKEN: I hate nobody and I love nobody. Now pick up that pin, hold it steady, and write down what I tell you.

[*She picks up the pen, grips it.*]

Dip it in the ink, it don't write dry.

[*She wets the pen.*]

Ready?

MYRTLE: Ready, my hand is steady.

CHICKEN: I got to be careful how I word this thing, it's too important for me to bugger it up.

MYRTLE: Let's make two copies of it, one for, for—practice and the other—final.

CHICKEN: Won't be necessary. I got it now. Now write down what I tell you in big letters or print. "Me, Mrs. Lot Ravenstock, if I had a claim on this place called Raven Roost or anything on this place give up and deny all claims when my husband is dead. Because this place goes to Chicken. I known about this setup before my TV marriage and the paper which Chicken holds with notary seal, two names of witnesses on it, still holds good. I declare this. The place and all on it will be Chicken's, all Chicken's, when Lot Ravenstock dies and also if I die too because of river in flood, a natural act of God."

MYRTLE [*who has been scribbling frantically*]: "All Chicken's when Lot dies."

CHICKEN: Now put in the punctuation and dot all the i's an' cross all the t's an' sign your name plain at the bottom.

MYRTLE: Yais, Yais, I did, I already did that, Chicken.

CHICKEN: Give it here. [*He takes the paper from her.*] Huh. I bet they never give you no spelling or handwriting prize when you went to school, but anyhow it's possible to read it if the question comes up in case of you being alive when the flood goes down. There's still one question, though. Where's the witnesses and the notary seal so this would hold up in court?

MYRTLE: Oh, we could get them later, we—!

CHICKEN: You wrote this thing because you're scared of drowning. How do I know you wouldn't back out of it when the flood's over with?

MYRTLE: I swear I wouldn't.

CHICKEN: Well, anyhow it's something, and something's better than nothing. It's worth putting in my wallet with Lot's witnessed letter and the true or false license.

MYRTLE: Chicken, trust my word. I've given you my word and never gone back on my word in all my life.

CHICKEN: I'm not counting on your word, but something else about you.

MYRTLE: What? Else? About me?

CHICKEN: —You're weak.

MYRTLE: I've always been weak compared to men, to a man. I think that's natural, don't you?

[*They have been sitting in chairs on opposite sides of the small, square kitchen table, chairs angled toward the audience. Now* CHICKEN *rises and moves close to her.*]

CHICKEN: Look me straight in the eyes and answer a question.

MYRTLE: What? Question?

CHICKEN: Can you kiss and like kissin' a man that's been accused of having some black blood in him?

MYRTLE: No! Yes! It would make no diff'rence to me.

CHICKEN: Let's try it out. Put your arms about me an' give me a kiss on the mouth. Mouth open.

[*She complies nervously, gingerly to this request. During the kiss, he puts a hand on her hips.*]

CHICKEN [*releasing her*]: —Well? How did it feel? Disgusting?

MYRTLE: No, not a bit. I was pleased an' relieved that you wanted to kiss me, Chicken.

CHICKEN: That kiss was just a beginning. You know that. Does that please and relieve you?

MYRTLE: I'm a warm-natured woman. You might say passionate, even. A Memphis doctor prescribed me a bottle of pills to keep down the heat of my nature, but those pills are worthless. Have no effect, I'm through with them. —Don't you know I would never back down on that letter you dictated to me? Not if I could, never would!

CHICKEN: No, I reckon you wouldn't.

[CHICKEN *hoists himself onto the kitchen table, directly in front of her, legs spread wide.*]

MYRTLE: Wouldn't you be more comf'tble in a chair?

CHICKEN: I wouldn' be as close to you. —I'm right in front of you now.

MYRTLE: That's a—high—table. I have to strain my neck to look in your face.

CHICKEN [*with a slow, savage grin*]: —You don't have to look in my face, my face ain't all they is to me. . . .

[*She begins suddenly to cry like a child.*]

Why're you cryin' fo' something you want an' can have?

[*He snatches up the lamp and blows it out. The kitchen is blacked out: an opaque scrim falls over its open wall. The light brightens in the bedroom where* LOT *sits in the wicker rocker; the moonlight on him brightens, fades, and brightens again.*]

LOT: Lamp's gone out in the kitchen and I don't hear a sound. —What I've done is deliver a woman to Chicken, brought home a whore for Chicken that he don't have to pay. —A present from the dying.

THE SCENE DIMS OUT.

SCENE SEVEN

The lights come up as CHICKEN *lights the lamp on the table. He is still perched on the table and* MYRTLE *is still on a chair so close to the table that she's between his boots, and she looks as if she had undergone an experience of exceptional nature and magnitude.*

CHICKEN: Let there be light. That's what they say that God said on the first day of creation.

[*Slight pause as he fastens the clasp of his belt.*]

MYRTLE: Chicken, I want you to know that—

CHICKEN: What do you want me to know that I don't know?

MYRTLE: That that's the first time I've gone that far with a man, no matter how strongly attracted.

CHICKEN: You mean on the first date?

MYRTLE: I mean practickly never.

CHICKEN: Maybe when instink is powerful enough, then practice is not necessary. But in my opinion, them little white tablets you take to keep your nature down you oughta send back to the Memphis doctor an' demand a refund on whatever they cost you.

MYRTLE: It's possible that the tablets are meant for ordinary attraction but not for terrific attraction.

CHICKEN: Like a levee holds back a river up till a point where the pressure is too strong for it?

MYRTLE: Yes, like that. Exackly.

[*She rises from her chair and makes a weak-kneed effort to climb on the table.*]

CHICKEN: What're you doin'?

MYRTLE: Tryin' to climb up beside you an' lean on your shoulder.

CHICKEN: Naw, naw, stay in your chair a while longer. I don't like to touch or be touched by a woman right after havin' such close relations with her.

MYRTLE [*returning to her chair, humbly*]: Are you disgusted with her?

CHICKEN: Just not int'rested in her.

MYRTLE: How long does that feelin' last?

CHICKEN: Sometimes five or tin minutes.

MYRTLE: Minutes kin seem like hours whin the attraction's terrific.

CHICKEN: —I wonder something about you.

MYRTLE [*nervously*]: Wh—what do you wonder?

CHICKEN: If the attraction wouid still be terrific if I was to tell you the talk an' suspicion about me are based on fact.

MYRTLE: —What, uh, talk an' suspicion?

CHICKEN: That I got colored blood in me.

[*Note:* MYRTLE *has the typical southern lower-class dread and awe of Negroes.*]

MYRTLE: Oh, I, why, I—I know they's no truth in that.

CHICKEN [*grinning at her savagely*]: How do you know they isn't?

MYRTLE: Lot would of *tole* me.

CHICKEN: I come near to killin' him once fo' sayin' I had colored blood an' Lot hasn't forgotten; he's not so dumb he don't know that if he told you, I'd know.

MYRTLE: Thin why would you tell me thet you—

CHICKEN: I thought you oughta know after havin' such close relations.

[*Shaken and awed by the disclosure, she rises from her chair and pulls it back from the table.*]

CHICKEN: Why'd you do that, Mrs. Lot Ravenstock?

MYRTLE: —Why'd I do what did I do, I—

CHICKEN: You moved your chair back from the table like a monster was on it.

MYRTLE: You wuh swingin' your boots with mud on 'em stainin' my blouse, and'—

CHICKEN: Your blouse was awready stained. Has to be washed in floodwater.

MYRTLE: Chicken, fo' God's sake, don't mention a possible flood to a girl scared as I am of water.

CHICKEN: Move your chair back where it was.

MYRTLE: I don't know where it was.

CHICKEN: Then what do you know? Nothin'?

[MYRTLE *moves her chair back to approximately its former position.*]

MYRTLE: Was it here?

CHICKEN: About. Now lissen to me. My mother had colored blood in her. She wasn't black but she wasn't white neither, and that's why I'm dark complected with freckled eyes an' live the life of a dawg that nobody owns and owns nothing. Ask any dawg on a road or a street, any dawg, any road, any street, if that ain't th' fuckin' truth which is made me suspicioned around here. So. Are you cryin' agin?

MYRTLE: —With, with—nervous—sympathy fo' you.

CHICKEN: Keep it, shove it, forget it. I don't want it. When you want sympathy, then is when you're in trouble. Up to your ass, up to your tits, up to your eyebrows in it, ask any dawg in the street, includin' you'self.

MYRTLE: Please don't talk thet way to me. [*She moves her chair back a little, still sniffling.*]

CHICKEN [*broodingly*]: One night last winter, for instance, I come up to this girl at the Dixie Star, a night-place on the highway. This girl I come up to politely was known as Desperate Dotty because she put out for men right and left and up the center an' down it.

MYRTLE: —No self-respeck?

CHICKEN: No self-respeck an' no white tablets from the quack in Memphis, but I was so horny that night my balls were achin', so I come up to this girl when the man she was with fell outa their booth to th' floor an' laid there belchin' an' snorin'. I spoke to this girl politely. "Hello, how are you, Miss Bows, terrible weather, and so forth." Then lowered my voice an' leaned on th' table toward her, an' said "Miss Bows, this man you're with here t'night cain't do you no good, any dawg on th' road can tell you that, so why not step over his laigs an' sit in a clean booth with me, I got almost a full pint of Four Roses on me." —What did I git fo' this polite invitation?

MYRTLE [*still sniffling*]: I don't, I should, I—

CHICKEN: I'll tell you what I got. She give me a quick, mean look an' said, "Nigger, stay in your place." That's it. That's how it is with me an' wimmen around here. Talk, suspicion, insult. An' when Miss Lottie, Lot's mother, dismissed me off this place, she said to me, "Chicken, I don't want my son to be known as half brother to a nigra." Wonderful, huh? Yeah, great. I'll tell you what her son does to amuse himself here. He gits in his dead mother's clothes—panties, brassiere, slippers, dress, an' a wig he made out of cornsilk. Ask any dawg in the street!

MYRTLE: —Oh, I—wouldn't ask any dawg a, a, a—thing like thet, I—

CHICKEN: Comes downstairs lookin' jus' like her an' sits in her parlor, talkin' to himself in the same voice as hers. OK? —Well, I'm back here, now, alone, suspicioned, despised.

MYRTLE: —I, uh—

CHICKEN: Oh, if I walk in town, I can go to the movies an' sit in th' white section an' watch a female actriss messin' around in a wrapper that you can almost see through. Shit, I've seen kids play with themselves at The Delta Brilliant an' I don't blame 'em. The movie industry is run by ole men with hot pants, you can ask any dawg in the street if that's not true. Pool hall, I can go to the pool hall, but nobody's anxious to git me in a game with 'em. Can go to the highway night-place, an' sit by myself, left out of the conversation, talked about in whispers. So what I do, practickly everything, I do by myself, you can ask any dawg that.

MYRTLE: You should, I would—pay no attention, rise above talk an' suspicion you know ain't true.

CHICKEN: I just now told you it was. Oh, but naw. You don't wanta believe it after the close relation we had between us, naw, your folks in Mobile wuh so ignorant an' low class they filtered your mind with the idea that you'd be ruined like poisoned by havin' a close relation to someone with colored blood. So? Yais, so. I know.

MYRTLE: I was just, just simply—I was surprised for a—minute, which is over with now.

CHICKEN: You're still holdin' onto th' arms of that chair with your haid leant back like you was about to be electrocuted.

MYRTLE: I been through a good deal t'day, more than some girls go through in their whole lifetimes.

CHICKEN: Like the Four Hot Shots from Mobile?

[*He gets off the table and moves to the back door which is the only solid enclosure of the set—the rest is created by lighting.*]

MYRTLE [*rising fearfully*]: Where are you goin'?

CHICKEN: The river's louder. I'm goin' to look at the levee.

MYRTLE: What good does it do to look at it?

CHICKEN: I can tell if the levee will hold the crest or not.

MYRTLE: Don't—

[*He goes off.*]

—leave me alone here. . . .

[*The bedroom upstairs is lighted by the moon.* LOT *is struggling out of the wicker rocker, knocking it over. He staggers to a closet and with his back to the audience, throws off the silk wrapper. He steps quickly into a gauzy white dress and sets a blond wig on his head. He turns around again, gasps, staggers to the foot of the brass bed and clings to its bars. Then he slides down them to a kneeling position.*]

LOT: —Will—make it—Miss Lottie! And order them both off the place!

[*The moon is obscured again and the bedroom returns to dark, a scrim descending over its front. During this,* MYRTLE *has stood at the open kitchen door. Now* CHICKEN *returns, hip boots covered with wet mud as when we first saw him.*]

MYRTLE: I thought you'd never git back here.

CHICKEN: You thought wrong, Missy.

[*He sits on the table again.*]

MYRTLE: —Those five or tin minutes are over with, now, ain't they?

CHICKEN: Cain't you see the clock?

MYRTLE: A clock is mechanical but a man is human.

CHICKEN: Sometimes you say a true thing.

MYRTLE: I pride myself on that, and another thing I pride myself on is noticin' an' appreciatin' a man's appearance. More, much more, than most girls I look at a man with appreciation. Physical. I notice such things about him as a strong figure in fine proportion. Mouth? Full. Teeth? White. Glist'nin'. Why, you look like a man that could hold back the flood of a river!

CHICKEN: No man can hold back a flood but some can live through one.

MYRTLE: —With a—with a woman?

CHICKEN: Uh-huh, even with a woman. —How'd you like to stay on here after Lot's gone?

MYRTLE: —Lit's not put it like thet.

CHICKEN: What other way would you put it?

MYRTLE: No, I don't know what other way I could put it. And I know thet ev'ry girl in the world has a dream in her heart that's sweeter an' more precicious to her than any other.

CHICKEN: What's that dream in her heart?

MYRTLE: That dream is settl'n' down somewhere, sometime, with a man to who she's very strongly attracted.

CHICKEN: Think it over an' I'll think it over, too. You're not a match fo' the pitcher tacked on the wall, but—

MYRTLE: No, no, but I—know!

CHICKEN: Yais, I'd say you know, an' if it's necessary to climb on the roof tonight, I'll git you up the ladder in the hall upstairs with a blanket in case we need more'n each other to keep us warm.

MYRTLE: What'd we eat up there if we had to stay up there long?

CHICKEN: The chickens'll fly up there, and if a helly-copter don't come over to pick us up, we'll drink some warm chicken blood to keep us goin'.

MYRTLE: Oh, I couldn't do that!

CHICKEN: What people have to do they always do. —So ev'rything understood now?

MYRTLE: I think we've come to a perfeck understandin'.

CHICKEN: Good. Let's have a drink on it. [*He pours liquor into two tin cups.*] —Have you ever been what they call saved?

MYRTLE: Why, yais, I have, I have been saved by you.

CHICKEN: What I was speakin' of is *religious* salvation.

[*He removes her importunate hand from his shoulder and resumes his seat on the table. The lamp light concentrates on him hotly during the monologue, the expression of his credo, that follows.* MYRTLE *is a shadowy presence.*]

MYRTLE: Oh, *religious* salvation.

CHICKEN: That's right.

MYRTLE: Well, I'm not a steady churchgoer, I wake up so tired on Sundays, y'see, but when I'm perplexed or worried over something, I always appeal to my Saviour and, knock on wood, He has never let me down.

[*The bright light is now fixed on* CHICKEN.]

CHICKEN: Hmm. Uh-huh. —I reckon you'd never guess from me, the way I am now, that I was what they call saved by this preacher Gypsy Smith when he come through here last Spring. But I sure in hell was, I was what they call saved, but it didn't last much longer than a cold in the head. Hmmm. And talking about salvation, I think there's a good deal of truth in the statement, the saying, that either you're saved or you ain't, and the best thing to do is find out which and stick to it. Because with human beings, and I'm a human being and you are, too, what counts most is—

[MYRTLE *perches herself beside him on the table and leans against him.*]

With human beings, the ones I known in my life, what counts most is personal satisfaction, and God knows you'll never get that by denying yourself what you want most in the world, by straining and struggling for what they call salvation when it's something you're just not cut out for. That preacher, that salvation preacher last spring, he claimed that we had to put up a terrible struggle against our lustful body. And I did for a while. Y'know, these preachers all think we got lustful bodies and that's one thing I know they're right about. Huh?

MYRTLE: Oh, yes. They're right about that. They're not mistaken.

CHICKEN: And they also believe that we have spiritual gates, and they preach about how you should haul down those spiritual gates on your lustful body. Well. Those are two opposite things and one of 'em's got to be stronger if they're in the same body. One's got to win and one lose. Well, I tried to haul down my spiritual gates for a while but I seemed to be reaching up for something that wasn't in me. You can't haul down your spiritual gates if you don't have any in you. I think that's the case in my case. I was just created without them. And either you're saved or you ain't, you can be or never will be, and I think you're a hell of a lot better off putting all hope of salvation out of your mind completely than to put up a long, painful struggle that's bound to be useless. Sooner or later, you're going to backslide, and that's that. Hmm? What do you think?

MYRTLE: In my case, I never had that experience, being saved, not even for a short while, but I do say prayers, anyhow, to God and to human beings.

CHICKEN: What do you pray for?

MYRTLE: I pray for protection, and right now I feel like that prayer is going to be answered. Go on talking in that deep voice of yours. I don't just hear it. It, it—it gives me a sensation in my ears and goes all through my body, it, it—it *vibrates* in me. I don't even hear the river!

CHICKEN [*with a touch of tolerant contempt*]: Mmm, mmm-hmmm. What you're saying is you're anxious to please me in order to git on the roof whin the house is flooded.

MYRTLE [*very nervously*]: Oh, no, that, that—that's already been settled.

CHICKEN: Things can be settled one way and then unsettled another.

MYRTLE: You wouldn't back out on it now after givin' your word, you couldn't, you're too good a man! God love you, Chicken!

CHICKEN: This house ain't built out of rock or brick or—cement. This is an old wood house. Oh, I'll git you up on the roof whin the levee collapses. But that's no guarantee that the crest of a flood of a river as big as this might not uproot this house like a weed and wash and toss it down and around till not a board or a shingle stuck together.

MYRTLE: Don't, don't—scare me out of my life!

CHICKEN [*sloshing liquor from the jug into their tin cups*]: I'll tell you how I look at life in my life, or in any man's life. There's nothing in the world, in this whole kingdom of earth, that can compare with one thing, and that one thing is what's able to happen between a man and a woman, just that thing, nothing more, is perfect. The rest is crap, all of the rest is almost nothing but crap. Just that one thing's good, and if you never had nothing else but that, no property, no success in the world, but still had *that*, why, then I say this life would still be worth something, and you better believe it. Yes, you could come home to a house like a shack, in blazing heat, and look for water and find not a drop to drink, and look for food and find not a single crumb of it. But if on the bed you seen you a woman waiting, maybe not very young or good-looking even, and she looked up at you and said to you "Daddy, I want it," why, then I say you got a square deal out of life, and whoever don't think so has just not had the right woman. That's how I look at it, that's how I see it now, in this kingdom of earth.

[LOT *appears like an apparition in the pool of cool light at the stair-top. He has put on the gauzy white dress to conjure an image of his mother in summer. As he stands above the stairs he puts on a translucent, wide "picture hat;" the crown is trimmed with faded flowers. The effect is both bizarre and beautiful. There is a phrase of music like a muted trumpet playing a blues song. Then* LOT *starts his descent of the stairs. With each step his gasping for breath is louder, but his agony is transfigured by the sexless passion of the transvestite. He has a fixed smile which is almost ecstatic.* CHICKEN *leaps off the kitchen table and goes to the kitchen door. He seems impressed but not surprised.* MYRTLE *is terrified.*]

MYRTLE: Chicken, Oh, God, stop him!

CHICKEN: What faw?

MYRTLE: Take him back up!

CHICKEN: Naw, naw, let him be in Miss Lottie's parlor.

[*At the foot of the stairs,* LOT *turns blindly towards the parlor. His gasping breath is now like a death rattle. Even in death he has the ecstasy of a transvestite. As he staggers into the bizarre little parlor, the room is lighted with a delicate rose light. There he stands swaying for a few moments; then sinks into one of the little gold chairs, facing the window.* MYRTLE *is panicky but not* CHICKEN. LOT, *in his transfiguration, stares blindly. He is even smiling as if on a social occasion. He holds onto his garden hat, holding it by the crown, as if a wind might blow it away. He is swaying back and forth.* CHICKEN'S *attitude is impassive.*]

—You're dressed fo' summer t'night.

[LOT *is past hearing any remark. He rises from the chair, sways, seems to bow to an applauding audience, then crumples to the floor.* CHICKEN *doesn't enter the parlor until* LOT'S *death agony is finished. Only then does he enter and sits gingerly on one of the gilt chairs for a moment. Then, almost tenderly, he moves the lifeless body to the sofa.* MYRTLE, *in a state of mental shock, has retreated to the kitchen and opened the icebox as if it were a place of refuge.*]

MYRTLE: Aigs. Bacon. Slab of it. New potatoes.

[*She removes these reassuring items from the iceless box. An egg or two splatters on the floor. She makes a few more rapid, irresolute turns.*]

Pan? —Pan! —Knife? —Knife!

[*She heads for the wall where these utensils are hanging and discovers her arms are full. Then she rushes back to deposit the foodstuff on the table. Entirely unnoticed by her, an egg or two more splatters on the floor. Then she rushes back to remove the utensils from their hooks.*]

In no condition to—got to!

[*She then instructs herself as if she were a pupil in a very primary cooking class.*]

Slice bacon in pan with knife. —Stove? —Burnin'!

[*Her words are interspersed with slight, breathless sobs.* CHICKEN *has stood over the summer gauze apparition of his half brother without a word or gesture. Now he turns out the chandelier and moves with dark satisfaction down the short hall to the kitchen area. He looks about him appraisingly, a man who has come into possessions fiercely desired.* MYRTLE'*s back is to him and when he speaks she catches her breath loudly.*]

CHICKEN: Makin' supper?

MYRTLE: What I'm doin' I don't know what I'm doin', I—

CHICKEN: You're doin' a sensible thing since it might be sev'ral days before we have a hot meal again.

MYRTLE [*turning to face him*]: Chicken, as Christian people—

CHICKEN: What about Christian people, something or nothing?

MYRTLE: We got to call in a doctor.

CHICKEN: If there was a doctor that hadn't hauled his ass out of Two River County, there's nothin' he could do here but clean up a mess of aigs you dropt on the floor.

MYRTLE: —Lot is—?

CHICKEN: Isn't.

MYRTLE: —God have mercy on my—

CHICKEN: What?

MYRTLE: —The potatoes will be home-fried.

CHICKEN: That's right. Fried in my home. You couldn't peel 'em?

MYRTLE: Cut my finger!

CHICKEN: A nervous woman has a rough time in this world.

[*He stares at her broodingly for a couple of moments as she sucks her cut finger.*]

I don't reckon that, no, I reckon you couldn't.

MYRTLE: Couldn't? What?

CHICKEN: Produce me a son. Produce a child for me, could you? I've always wanted a child from an all-white woman.

MYRTLE: —I want t' be perfeckly frank with you on that subjeck.

CHICKEN: I could tell if you lied on that subjeck or any other.

[*He holds the lamp toward her still panicky face.*]

MYRTLE: I got five adopted children.

CHICKEN: You adopted five children?

MYRTLE: No, what I mean is, Chicken, I hed five children that hed t' be adopted because I wasn' financially able to give these children the care an' attention—an' care a infant child's got t' have, an' so I hed t' hev 'em adopted, all by families with yearly incomes no less 'n two thousan' dollars. Oh, it broke my heart five times. All five was red-headed like me an' cute as a bug.

CHICKEN: I don't want a child that looks like a bug.

MYRTLE: Oh, that's just a, you know, a—expression.

[*He replaces the lamp on the table.*]

No, sir. The deepest chord in my nature is the— Don't that river sound louder? Or am I just more scared to death of it?

CHICKEN: The flood crest is close to here now. [*He starts outside.*]

MYRTLE [*wildly*]: *Don't leave me alone here!*

CHICKEN: I'm goin' out th' door for a minute. Sit down. Peel the home-fried potatoes. —I want to look at my land. [*He goes out and moves forward, his face exultant.*]
—*Sing it out, frogs an' crickets, Chicken is king!*

[MYRTLE *has come out behind him. There is a great booming sound.*]

Up! Quick!

[*He says this as the curtain is descending.*]

END.